VICIOUS CIRCLES AND OTHER SAVAGE SHAPES

·MURDEROUS **MATHS**·

JOIN THE MURDEROUS MATHS GANG
FOR MORE FUN, GAMES AND TIPS AT
www.murderousmaths.co.uk

.MURDEROUS MATHS.

VICIOUS CIRCLES AND OTHER SAVAGE SHAPES

KJARTAN POSKITT

Illustrated by
Philip Reeve

Hippo

To my old friend Merlin. He spent eleven years of morning walks listening to me and never complained once.

Scholastic Children's Books,
Euston House, 24 Eversholt Street,
London NW1 1DB, UK
a division of Scholastic Ltd
London ~ New York ~ Toronto ~ Sydney ~ Auckland
Mexico City ~ New Delhi ~ Hong Kong

First Published by Scholastic Ltd, 2002

Acknowledgements: Thanks to David Mitchell, Liz Meenan and
Rob Eastaway for their advice on some of the articles in this book.

10 digit ISBN 0 439 99747 X
13 digit ISBN 978 0439 99747 8

All rights reserved
Typeset by TW Typesetting, Midsomer Norton, Somerset
Printed and bound by Nørhaven Paperback A/S, Denmark

10 9

CONTENTS

THE SECRET VAULT

…inside the lifts in the Murderous Maths building there are about 50 buttons to take you to all the different floors. Admittedly that's not a terribly exciting bit of news, but as you've taken the time to join us in another Murderous Maths book, we'll let you in on a secret! If you push buttons 7, 35 and 43 all at the same time, the lift takes you *down* to a secret level well below the basement. As it's going to take us a few minutes to get there, we'll explain what's special about it…

The no number zone

Most of maths uses lots of numbers, some letters, a handful of signs and a few odd squiggles that no one is absolutely sure about. However, the secret vault is full of the most murderous maths that doesn't use numbers at all! And no numbers means…

It's true. All you're going to need on this trip are a few drawings and a good imagination! Be honest, even if you're one of those people who loves crunching, smashing and mincing big sums to bits, you've got to admit that now and then it would be nice to do something different.

One of the greatest maths brains of all time was Isaac Newton (the apple-on-head, "ouch-oh-hey-I've-just-discovered-gravity" bloke) and although he used to do sums that were miles long, even HE admitted...

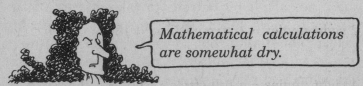

> *Mathematical calculations are somewhat dry.*

So put away your nasty little calculator, because you won't need it. You won't even need to count on your fingers, so you can wear boxing gloves if you like. What you WILL find useful are:

- One or two decent pencils. (A few nicely sharpened coloured pencils makes it even more fun.)
- A ruler to draw straight lines. (But we won't look at the numbers on it.)
- A pair of compasses.
- A pair of scissors.
- Some clean paper. Squared paper can make life easier for quickly drawing rectangles or lines of an exact length.

And these might also come in handy:

- A 45° set square.
- A 60° set square.
- A protractor.

Angles

We won't be measuring any lengths, but we will need to know about some angles. People used to base the measurements of angles on the right angle – which you can also call a "quarter turn". These days we use degrees which have a little sign like this °. Here's how they all fit together:

1 right angle = 1 quarter turn = 90° =

2 right angles = 1 straight line = 180°=

4 right angles = a full circle = 360° =

So what's this all about?

We're going to be dealing with **shape**. In the olden days it was known as geometry, and most of what we'll be concerned with is finding out when angles are the same size, lines are the same length and shapes have the same area. So keep your wits about you as the lift comes to a stop...

When you step out you'll find yourself in a double maximum top security restricted area! The temperature and humidity are precisely monitored, the floor, walls and ceiling are made of soft rubber to absorb any draughts or vibrations, and any stray flies are immediately zapped by laser beams.

When the Ancient Greeks first studied maths, their favourite subject was shape. That's why so many of their discoveries came from studying mathematical drawings. Some of these drawings were done using ink and paper, but a lot of them were simply traced out in sand on the ground. Luckily for us, followers of the great maths brains such as Pythagoras and Archimedes would sneak round at the end of the day and very carefully slide a tray under the sand with the drawings on, and that way they could carefully carry these priceless originals home and show their friends. The miracle is that despite wars, earthquakes, winds and rain, some of these diagrams have actually survived intact for thousands of years and finally they've ended up in our secret vault!

Here is one of the simplest diagrams. It shows one of the most important rules of shape:

Yes indeed. "Isosceles" actually means "equal legs" and in an isosceles triangle, the two angles opposite the equal sides always have to be the same size. It doesn't matter if the triangle is a long pointy one or a short flat one. The fun bit is that it's maths but there are no numbers involved!

This diagram dates back many thousands of years, so isn't it amazing to think that not one single grain of sand has moved in all that time!

A test drive...

Before we dive into triangles, polygons, circle stuff, origami and everything, let's try and recreate one of the sand diagrams we've just accidentally trashed in the secret vault. The Ancient Greek genius Thales claimed that "any angle drawn in a semicircle is always a right angle".

Oh dear. Even if we don't have any sums to do, there are going to be other challenges facing us. A lot of them are to do with proving why some things simply *have* to be true. Let's test this Thales rule first and see how we get on...

- Draw a line, then stick your compasses in the middle and draw a semicircle to sit on the line. Let's call the points where the line meets the semicircle M and S for Meets Semicircle. (Why not? You can use any letters you like.)

- Pick *any point you like* on the semicircle and call it Janet. (Why just use letters?) Janet can be right in the middle, or she can be down by M or over by S.

- Draw a straight line from Janet to M and another straight line from Janet to S.

- Check the angle at Janet. It will always be a right angle! (A set square is useful for checking right angles.)

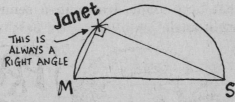

And now, thanks to Thales, Murderous Maths is proud to present:

A RATHER MESSY AND COMPLETELY USELESS WAY OF DRAWING A SEMI-CIRCLE USING A SET SQUARE:

1 Get a flat surface that nobody minds you pushing pins into.

2 Push in two pins. The gap between them should be slightly less than the shortest side of your set square.

3 Lightly sprinkle some flour or soot or sand evenly across the surface.*

4 Slide your set square up to the pins so that the two shorter sides are each touching a pin.

5 Keeping the two sides in contact with the pins, turn the set square backwards and forwards so that it clears a pattern in the flour, soot or sand.

6 The pattern will be a perfect semicircle!

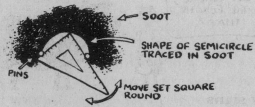

*Handy hint: if you are doing a posh exam and you need to hand your semicircle in to be marked, sprinkle the surface with wet cement powder then blow it with a hairdryer when you've finished.

As you can see, Thales' rule always seems to work.

He's right. What we need to do is show that Thales' rule always HAS to work, but that requires expert knowledge. So with your permission, m'lud, the case is adjourned until page 113.

A vicious half circle
Thales was so pleased about angles in semicircles that he decided to celebrate in real style. He had a bull dragged to an altar and sacrificed. But don't worry. If you get a maths question correct, you can make do with a neat little tick by the answer. You don't need to go round disembowelling cattle.

A few signs
In this book, we'll be looking at lots of cute diagrams with angles, curves, lines and so on. To show what's going on, there are three signs you need to know:

EQUAL LENGTHS
The short lines are the same length, and they are marked with a single dash. The longer lines are also equal, but as they are different from the short lines, they are marked with a double dash.

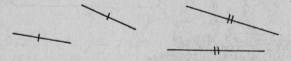

PARALLEL LINES
The lines with one arrow head are PARALLEL to each other. (It doesn't matter if they are different

lengths.) This means you can draw them for ever and they will always be the same distance apart – just like the rails on a straight piece of train track. The lines with two arrowheads are also parallel.

EQUAL ANGLES

When angles are equal, they can either be marked with the same letter, or they can be marked with a little arc inside them. (We've seen these arc signs already on the isosceles triangle.) If there are more than one set of equal angles then we use a double arc for the second set, and a triple arc if there's a third set, and so on.

One of the Ancient Greek rules is that when two lines cross, the **opposite angles** are equal. What's more, if a line crosses two parallel lines, you get equal angles called **corresponding angles**.

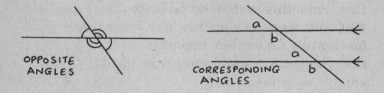

If you want to go a bit crazy, you could draw two pairs of parallel lines that cross each other. The shape in the middle is called a "parallelogram". The good bit is that if you mark ALL the equal sides and angles, it would look like this...

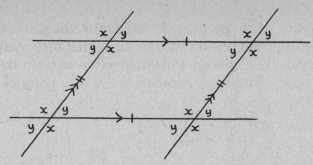

So now you know what to do next time it's a miserable rainy afternoon.

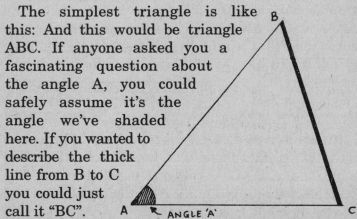

NO, IT'S STILL NOT QUITE MISERABLE ENOUGH FOR THAT.

Labelling shapes, lines and angles

Quite often a diagram has lots of letters on it which are used to describe different bits.

The simplest triangle is like this: And this would be triangle ABC. If anyone asked you a fascinating question about the angle A, you could safely assume it's the angle we've shaded here. If you wanted to describe the thick line from B to C you could just call it "BC".

B

A   ANGLE 'A'   C

When you get more complicated diagrams you have to be more careful...

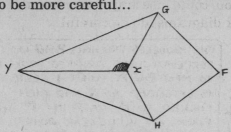

It's obvious where line FG is, and there are no prizes for guessing which shape is triangle HXY. But how would you describe the shaded angle? You can't just say angle "X" because there are three angles there! The foolproof way to write it is like this: GX̂Y. You'll see the X is in the middle wearing a little paper hat. That means the angle is at point X. The G and Y tell you which lines the angle is between. Otherwise you can write it like this: <GXY.

Sometimes people are in such a mad rush that they don't bother wasting time with the little hat. They would just call the angle "GXY", but the trouble is it might not be clear if they mean the angle or the whole GXY triangle. It's this sort of confusion that could bring the whole country grinding to a halt, so it's better to make the effort.

A final warning

Although you could use any letters or names you like to mark diagrams, do be careful…

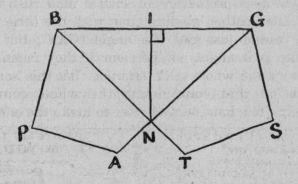

THE ISOCELES TRIANGLE **BNG** HAS A PERPENDICULAR DROPPED FROM **N** TO MEET **BG** AT POINT **I**. LINE **GN** IS EXTENDED TO **A** AND THEN LINKED TO **B** VIA POINT **P** TO FORM AN IRREGULAR QUADRILATERAL. LIKEWISE **BN** IS EXTENDED TO **T** AND THEN LINKED TO **G** VIA POINT **S** SO THAT QUADRILATERALS **BNAP** AND **GNTS** ARE CONGRUENT.

It all sounds rather posh and impressive doesn't it? However, when you look at the diagram…

LOCUS, FOCUS AND A BIT OF HOCUS POCUS

As you probably know, the distance from the centre of a circle to the edge is called the **radius** of the circle. But if you have an evil teacher who's feeling a bit nasty, you might fall into this trap...

Sadly he's right. This is because radius is a word from the ancient language, Latin, and it means ... well, radius actually. The trouble is that Latin words can have lots of different endings depending on how they fit into sentences. Just one radius ends in "us" but if you have more than one the "us" turns into "i". That's how come you end up with a word that has double letter "i" at the end. Weird or what? Mind you, "radii" comes up in crosswords quite a lot, so remember it if ever you're stuck.

Here's the good bit. Just about any old teacher knows about radius and radii, but that's only half the story. If they want to *really* get their Latin correct, they should know ALL the possible endings of radius. If you measure just one radius, to be absolutely technical you should say, "I'm going to measure the radium." Posh, eh? But if we use a bit of hocus pocus and travel back in time a few minutes, here's what you *could* have said about measuring more than one radius...

What's better is that the conversation could continue like this:

It's a nice thought, isn't it? But for now we'll just stick to "radius" and "radii".

We're about to come across locus and loci and later in the ellipses chapter there's focus and foci, but in the meantime don't make this mistake...

21

Loci

A locus is the name we give to a lot of tiny points that all obey the same rule. This sounds pretty grim, but it's dead easy. Suppose you have a circle with a little cross in the centre: every point on the circle has to be the same distance from the centre. In fact, instead of calling it a circle, we could call it *the locus of all the points that are the same distance from the cross*! Mind you, "circle" is catchier.

The perpendicular bisector

Here's a locus problem... The terribly lovely Veronica Gumfloss is dashing home to meet her hunky Australian cousin, but as she's about to cut across the playing fields, she spots Wayne Wayneson on one side and Rodney Tuft on the other. They are both looking hopefully in her direction, and she knows that whoever she passes closer to will immediately assume he's been invited to walk her back for a long smooch on her front doorstep. This would never normally be a problem to Veronica, but today – with a hunky Australian available – *no thanks, boys!*

So what route should Veronica take to make sure she is always exactly the same distance from both Wayne and Rodney?

What we want here is the locus of all points equidistant (i.e. the same distance) from both Rodney and Wayne. You might think this involves taking lots of measurements and dividing by 2, but no! Look at this:

- Draw a plan showing Wayne and Rodney.
- Stick the point of your compasses on to Wayne and then open then up to a bit more than halfway to Rodney. Draw an arc. (An arc is a bit of a circle)
- *Keep Your Compasses Open Exactly The Same Distance* ... and then stick the point on to Rodney. Draw a second arc to cut the first one in two places.
- Finally use the ruler to draw a straight line that goes through the two places where the arcs cross.

If you pick any point on this line, you'll find it's exactly the same distance from both Rodney and Wayne – so the line is Veronica's safest path!

23

This simple drawing trick has another use. If you already have a straight line drawn, you can split it into two equal halves with a second line that cuts it at 90°.

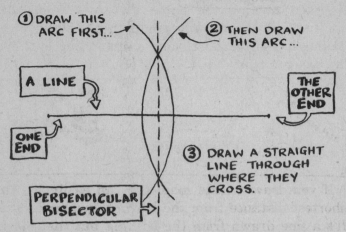

The diagram explains it all. Just make sure that your compasses are open exactly the same amount for drawing each arc. This new line has a dead posh name – because it bisects the line (i.e. chops it in half) at a perpendicular angle (i.e. 90°) it's called a **perpendicular bisector**.

Dropping a perpendicular

Colonel Fogsworth has been taking a dip at Brownpool-by-the-Sea in a costume knitted by the Duchess. Unfortunately, a loose strand got caught on a passing dredger and now he finds himself completely starkers in the water wondering how to get back to his bathing hut at the back of the beach. Luckily, you're on hand to help out with a bit of Murderous Maths. Obviously, though, he's going to have to do a quick chilly sprint, but what would be his shortest route from the sea to the bathing hut?

If you draw a little map, you can easily see the shortest distance from the bathing hut to the sea. It's a line drawn from the bathing hut that meets the edge of the sea at right angles. If you want to draw this line in accurately, it's called "dropping a perpendicular" and in this case we're dropping it from the bathing hut to the edge of the sea.

- Stick your compass point on the bathing hut.
- Open your compasses so they reach past the edge of the sea. Draw an arc that cuts the edge of the sea twice. We'll call these points N and C (for Naked Colonel).

- Construct the perpendicular bisector of the edge of the sea in between N and C.
- Here's the fun bit! If you've got it absolutely right, you should find the bisector goes up and hits the bathing hut.

There! You've dropped the perpendicular from the hut to the sea, and that shows the Colonel's shortest path to run and get dressed.

(This problem shows one of the great advantages of knowing a bit of maths. If you didn't know about dropping perpendiculars, then instead you'd have had to offer to fetch him a towel which wouldn't be nearly as funny.)

Bisecting angles

You've just been revving your cosmic phazmazycle around the chasms of the planet Goar. Wahey! Suddenly you find yourself shooting out of a ferric canyon which is getting wider and wider, but your status display indicates that the walls of the canyon are magnetic. You must find a path that goes exactly between the two walls – one false move and your zycle will be dragged over to the side and splattered,

26

with you on it. Time to lower your acti-screen visor and create a computer map.

What you need to know is *the locus of points equidistant from the two walls*. This sounds a bit grim, but luckily it's much easier to draw than say. What you need to do is bisect the angle between the two walls.

- Stick your compass point in where the lines meet. Open it up and draw an arc that cuts both lines. We'll call these points S and P (for Splattered Phazmazyclist).

- Now put the compass point on S and draw an arc in the middle of the gap between the two lines.
- *Keep your compasses open exactly the same distance* and put the point on P. Draw an arc to chop the last one.
- Join the point where the arcs meet to the point of the angle.

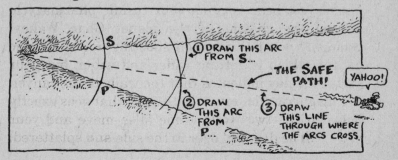

The line you've just drawn has chopped the angle exactly in half – and that's the path you should take.

Well done! You've learnt a few nifty things to do with your compasses, you've found out what loci are and you've picked up a handy bit of conversational Latin. There's a fancier locus to play with in the chapter on ellipses, but just before we move on, have a look at this secret code word ... KYCOETSD

We'll be using it several times in the book to save space, so can you work out what it means? To find out, look back over the past few pages. Clue: the "C" stands for "compasses".

EVERYTHING WORTH KNOWING ABOUT TRIANGLES

Triangles have *three* sides, *three* corners, there are *three* different sorts and the most important thing about them is *three* words long:

TRIANGLES DON'T COLLAPSE

To understand this fully, let's catch up with Pongo McWhiffy who has somehow cajoled the terribly lovely Veronica Gumfloss into joining him on a picnic.

So, being the perfect gentleman, Pongo offers to construct a seat for Veronica. He grabs four sturdy branches and, pulling a hammer and nails from his pocket, he knocks them together into a nice square shape for her to sit on.

If only Pongo had used a triangle instead!

A three-sided shape will always stay the same even if it's hinged at the corners, but if a shape has more than three sides it can flop about all over the place. If you look at an electricity pylon, you'll see that the whole structure is one very complicated shape broken into lots of small shapes. Most of these small shapes are triangles which is what makes the pylon solid enough to stand up. If all the small shapes were squares or rectangles, one decent puff of wind and the whole great big expensive electricity pylon would just fold up and plop down to the ground with a big fizzuppa kazzapp. (Which would be very very serious so don't laugh.)

When it comes to shapes on paper, any shape with straight sides can be split up into triangles, and quite often that's a useful thing to do as we'll see later. In the meantime let's find out all the exciting stuff there is to know about triangles.

The three different sorts of triangle

EQUILATERAL TRIANGLES
All three sides are the same length and all three angles are equal. If we were going to worry about numbers we would say that each angle is 60°, but we weren't so we won't.

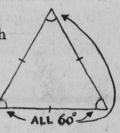

ALL 60°

ISOSCELES TRIANGLES
Two sides are the same length, and the angles opposite these sides are equal.

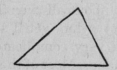

SCALENE TRIANGLES
All sides are a different length and all the angles are different.

There are a few other things to say about a triangle:
● If the biggest angle is a right angle then it's a right-angled triangle.

31

- If the biggest angle is bigger than a right angle, then it's an "obtuse" triangle.
- If all the angles are smaller than right angles then it's an "acute" triangle.

SOME OTHER INTERESTING TRIANGLES

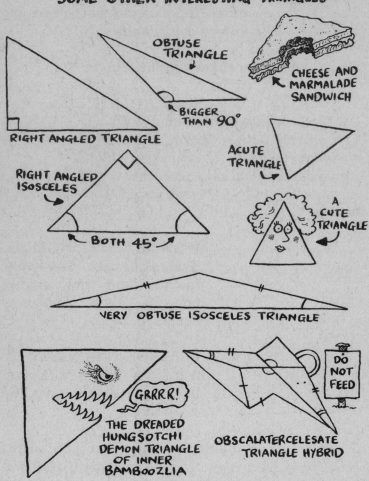

OBTUSE TRIANGLE

BIGGER THAN 90°

CHEESE AND MARMALADE SANDWICH

RIGHT ANGLED TRIANGLE

ACUTE TRIANGLE

RIGHT ANGLED ISOSCELES

BOTH 45°

A CUTE TRIANGLE

VERY OBTUSE ISOSCELES TRIANGLE

GRRRR!

THE DREADED HUNGSOTCHI DEMON TRIANGLE OF INNER BAMBOOZLIA

DO NOT FEED

OBSCALATERCELESATE TRIANGLE HYBRID

Triangle angles

If you cut ANY shape of triangle out of a piece of paper and tear the corners off, you can always put them together to make a straight line.

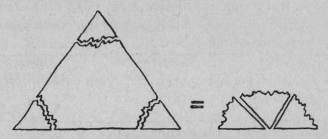

This is because the three angles together always add up to 180° or, if you prefer, two right angles.

A variation of this trick is to cut a right-angled triangle out of paper (you could just cut the corner off a normal sheet of paper to do this). Tear off the two smaller angles and you'll find that you can always fit them exactly over the right angle. This shows that in a right-angled triangle the two smaller angles always add up to 90°.

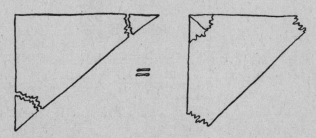

Are you a triangle fanatic?

If you want to know how much triangles really mean to you, have a look at the following statements. Are they true or false?

33

- A scalene triangle can be right-angled.
- A right-angled triangle cannot be obtuse.
- Your perfect valentine card has a big triangle on the front.

- An isosceles triangle cannot have three different angles.
- You live in a pyramid.

- Equilateral triangles must be acute.
- Some right-angled triangles are isosceles.
- The smartest thing you could ever wear is a hat folded out of newspaper.

- Sandwiches must be cut diagonally – and NEVER into squares.

- You cannot draw a triangle on a flat piece of paper with more than one right angle.
- A triangle isn't just for maths, it's for life.

Now check your answers:

All false: Obviously triangles have no beauty or inner meaning for you. What a tragic waste of a brain.

Some true: In the distant darkness of your soul, there flickers a small triangular light. Have hope.

Mostly true: You are a happy, enlightened, well-balanced person who doesn't care if other people snigger when your back is turned.

All true: Take a cold shower. This chapter is going to be TOO MUCH for you, you nutcase.

One person who would need a cold shower at this point would have been the Hungarian composer Franz Liszt because he was extremely fond of his musical triangle. (You've probably had a bash on one yourself at some point. It's like a shiny metal rod that's bent into an equilateral triangle shape and it goes "ting" when you hit it. As an instrument it might seem a bit humble compared to things like trombones and cellos, but if you're standing at the back of a big orchestra, adding the odd "ting" in the right place makes all the difference.)

In 1849 Franz wrote his first concerto for piano, but at one point the instructions say that the piano has to belt up so that everybody can hear the triangle do a solo. For triangle fans, this is undoubtedly the most tuneful and moving piece of music ever written.

NOW THAT'S WHAT I CALL MUSIC!

TING!

Why does a milking stool only have three legs?

...BECAUSE THE COW'S GOT THE UDDER ONE!

Oh, ha, ha, very funny. That was supposed to be a serious question. Now let's mooove on...

One of the odd things about triangles is that you can't twist them. Here's an experiment to explain this:

- Get some pencils or other long straight things.
- Fix the ends of four pencils together to make a four-sided shape such as a rectangle. (Use some tape or Blu-tack.)
- Hold two opposite sides of your shape and give it a bit of a twist. Easy enough, isn't it? If you lie it down on a flat tabletop, one corner could be sticking right up in the air.
- Now fix three of your pencils into a triangle.
- Can you twist it? No, you can't. The triangle will always be "flat". If you put it on the table, all three corners will touch the surface.

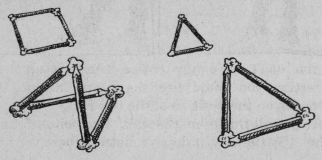

There's a reason for this. The posh way to say it is: "two points define a line" and "three points define a plane" but as it sounds a bit vague, let's pop down to the Murderous Maths weapons depot and get ourselves geared up for an experiment.

Suppose you see two tiny flies hovering in the air.

You could borrow a laser beam which fires a very thin beam of light in a straight line. Using the laser you could bore a hole through both flies at the same time, providing you pointed it in exactly the right direction. Even if the flies move, you should still be able to zap them both in one go so long as you move the beam to the right place.

You don't have any choice, there is only one direction you could fire the beam in and that depends on the position of the two flies.

To put all this in mathspeak, "two points define a line". (By the way, it doesn't matter where your two points are – one could be stuck under your fridge and the other on the planet Venus, it's always possible to join them up with one straight line.)

The two flies call up reinforcements and to your horror, a third tiny fly appears.

If you're really lucky, you might find all three flies are in a straight line, but it's not very likely.

However, our weapons depot can also issue you with a very long, very wide and very, VERY thin sheet of glass. Ha! Now you've got 'em. It doesn't matter where your three flies are, providing you tip the glass to exactly the right angle and fire it through the air from exactly the right position, you can slice all the flies in half at once.

In this case the glass sheet is a "plane" which is a very big flat thing. If you have three points, you can always fit them on the same plane providing it's tilted to the correct angle.

So, back to the milking stool.

If you want to put a normal four-legged chair on a floor without it rocking, you need to find four points for it to stand on which are on the same plane. Any decent floor is completely flat, so finding four points on the same plane is easy because any four points on the floor will do. But as you are doubtless aware, the floor of a cowshed isn't always a smooth flat plane; it could be quite uneven. Finding four points on the same plane for the chair to rest on could be very hard, and the chances are that one leg will not make contact. The whole thing would rock and next thing you know, you'd be falling over backwards into something brown while still clutching Buttercup's udders.

However, the three-legged milking stool only needs to touch the floor at three points. Because ANY three points are always on the same plane, it doesn't matter how uneven the floor is, the three points where the legs touch it are on a plane. Therefore you can put the stool safely anywhere without it rocking. So no rocking, no falling, no smelly laundry and no cow making a strangled screeching-cow noise.

When are triangles the same?

When people are drawing out maps or measuring the heights of flag-poles or just generally hanging out in the wacky world of triangles, it's handy to know when two triangles are exactly the same. In the maths trade we say they are **congruent** which means they are the same size, same shape, have the same area and share the same triangle interests such as going to the opera or belonging to a swimming club.

If you were testing two people to find out if they were congruent, you'd need to ask about a million questions, and even if all the answers were exactly the same, you'd probably still find some little detail that was different, such as one of them doesn't like spinach.

Luckily, with triangles you only need to check three of the details, and if they match up, then you know that everything else MUST be the same.

What's even better is that you've a few choices.

You know that two triangles are congruent:
IF you know that all three sides are the same length
for both triangles.

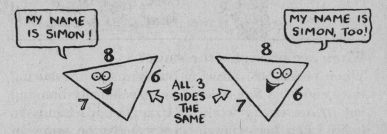

OR you know one side is the same for both triangles
and the angles at each end of that side are the same.

NOTICE TRIANGLES CAN BE 'TURNED OVER' BUT ARE STILL CONGRUENT.

OR you know that two of the sides are the same,
and the angle between them is the same. (This is
called the **included** angle.)

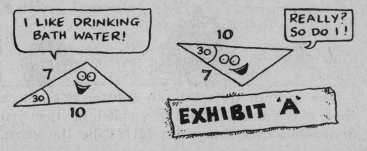

BUT watch out if you know that two of the sides are the same and one of the angles NOT between them is the same! (This is an **excluded** angle.)

It's an easy mistake to make, as the great detective Sheerluck Homes found to his cost. He was sent a description of a trouser-thieving triangle that read as follows:

$$AB = 16 \quad AC = 11 \quad <ABC = 30°.$$

As you can see, the same description fits two completely different triangles and Sheerluck nabbed the wrong one! So in future, Sheerluck, make sure that the angle is *included*.

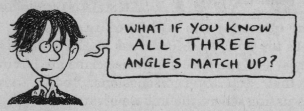

If all the angles match up, the triangles are called similar. It's possible that they are also congruent, but this is more likely:

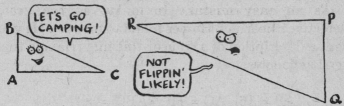

Even if you know angle A = P and B = Q and C = R, you'll notice that one triangle is a lot bigger than the other. Therefore they are not congruent. In fact they have different lengths of sides, different areas and probably wildly differing lifestyles and personal goals.

Knowing when triangles are congruent can suddenly come in useful in all sorts of odd ways as you'll find out later in this book. As for similar triangles, they have lots of special uses – one of them is the "shadow stick" which is described in *Murderous Maths: Desperate Measures*.

The quest for the middle of a triangle

Let's nip up to the Murderous Maths testing laboratory where the pure mathematicians are having one of their top level discussions. Today they are discussing where the middle of a triangle is.

IF YOU START WITH ANY TRIANGLE, YOU CAN FIND THE AREA BY SPLITTING IT INTO TWO RIGHT-ANGLED TRIANGLES. HERE I'VE DROPPED A PERPENDICULAR FROM A DOWN TO BC. THE EXCITING BIT IS THAT IF I DROP A PERPENDICULAR FROM C TO AB AND ONE FROM B TO AC, THEY ALL CROSS IN THE SAME PLACE SO THIS MUST BE THE CENTRE!

NO! IF YOU BISECT ALL THE ANGLES YO'ULL FIND THAT ALL THREE LINES CROSS IN THE SAME PLACE. WHAT'S MORE, IF YOU DRAW A CIRCLE THAT FITS EXACTLY INSIDE THE TRIANGLE, THAT'S WHERE THE MIDDLE OF THE CIRCLE COMES!

NO! IF YOU DRAW PERPENDICULAR BISECTORS FOR EACH SIDE, THESE ALL CROSS IN THE SAME PLACE, EVEN IF IT'S OUTSIDE THE TRIANGLE! AND IF YOU DRAW A CIRCLE TO TOUCH ALL THREE CORNERS, THAT'S WHERE THE CENTRE OF THE CIRCLE IS.

44

RUBBISH! JOIN EACH CORNER TO THE MIDDLE OF THE OPPOSITE LINE AND YOU'LL FIND YOUR THREE LINES ALL CROSS IN THE SAME PLACE. AND WHAT'S MORE...

... THE TRIANGLE BALANCES EXACTLY ON THAT POINT, BECAUSE IT'S THE CENTRE OF GRAVITY.

I'VE GOT THE EXACT CENTRE!

NO WAY! MINE'S RIGHT!

GNOFF!

SPLAFF!

For goodness' sake! The only way to settle them down is to get an equilateral triangle and let them all have a go on it. By the time they'd finished this is what they'd get:

Now that they've all agreed on the same centre, maybe they'll give us a hand with something else...

When triangles have the same area

If triangles have the same base and the same height, then they have the same area.

For instance the triangles printed here all cover exactly the same amount of paper...

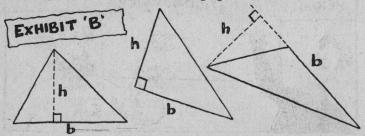

All you have to check is that the height is measured at right angles to whichever side you choose as the base. You'll notice that with the obtuse triangle, the height measurement is actually *outside* the triangle.

Of course, self-respecting Murderous Maths readers don't like just to be told things, they like to check it for themselves. However, if you think this one looks a bit tough then don't worry! It's rather fun because we're going to make some little jigsaw puzzles in a minute.

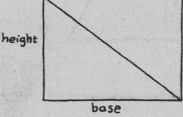

Look at this diagram of a rectangle. It's got a diagonal across it which splits it into two triangles which are exactly the same (or *congruent*). It doesn't take a lot of imagination to see that each triangle covers exactly half the rectangle.

Yes, if you've read *Desperate Measures* you'll know these formulas, but we're trying to avoid stuff like multiplying and dividing in this book. So instead of sums and calculators, we'll test this out with scissors and paper. Hooray.

Here's the clever bit. Suppose you move the top of the triangle along a bit like this...

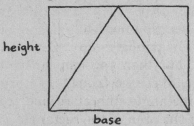

This new triangle still covers up exactly half the rectangle! Let's prove it.

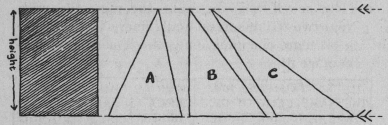

Make TWO big copies of this diagram. (It's very easy if you've got squared paper.) All you need to do is draw two long parallel lines, and then mark in the three triangles and the rectangle. Make sure the lengths of all the bases are exactly the same. The top of the triangles A and B can be anywhere above their bases, and the top of C should be somewhere off to the side, like Mr Reeve's done it here.

What we're going to show is that each triangle has exactly half the area of the shaded rectangle.

Therefore all three triangles have the same area as each other!

- Cut out both your "A" triangles. The idea is to put them together so that they cover the rectangle exactly. This diagram shows you what to do...

- As you can see, you need to chop one of the triangles up the middle, but then you can make the correct shape. As it takes two triangles to exactly cover the whole rectangle, therefore one triangle has exactly *half* the area of the rectangle.

- If you try with your two "B" triangles, you should find you can do the same thing.

- Now, see if you can make the rectangle with your two "C" triangles! You'll find you need to do a bit more chopping, but you should be able to manage it!

ALL THE TRIANGLES HAD THE SAME LENGTH OF BASE AND THE SAME HEIGHT. THIS EXPERIMENT SHOWS THAT THIS MAKES THEIR AREAS EQUAL.

AND AS THE RECTANGLE AREA IS 'BASE TIMES HEIGHT', EACH TRIANGLE HAS THE AREA 'HALF BASE × HEIGHT'.

Triangles with the same area sneak up on you in all sorts of different ways. If you have parallel lines such as the sides of a ladder, this can happen...

The length of the base is the same in each case, and the height is the same, so they all have the same area.

Here's the window in the Pure Mathematicians' testing laboratory. It's divided into four equal panes, but look at the cobwebs:

The long thin cobweb only has half the base, but it does have twice the height of the other one. It turns out the cobwebs are exactly the same size!

The cake-cutting crisis

You might think we've gone a bit over the top with all this "equal triangle area" stuff, but sometimes it can be a matter of life or death...

City:	Chicago, Illinois, USA
Place:	Luigi's Diner, Upper Main Street
Date:	15 May 1929
Time:	9:10 p.m.

It wasn't tuneful, it wasn't sincere and it wasn't even appreciated. Benni the waiter fell silent as the the seven stony faces around the central table stared at him.

A few minutes before, he had been in the kitchen helping his boss prepare the biggest cake ever seen in the state. The trolley that carried it had been converted from an old railway truck, and the metal wheels had already driven grooves into the floor.

"Sing to the man," Luigi, his boss, had told him. "It's the big guy's birthday, and they're our best customers."

"That's because they're our only customers," Benni had replied. "They scare everybody else away."

"They scare me away," admitted Luigi. "The trouble is, this is my place and I've nowhere else to scare away to. Boy, I hate it when the Gabriannis and the Boccellis try to get along together. It's supposed to be a birthday party and yet they've just stared each other out all  evening. If we don't lighten the mood, then the lead's gonna start flying. So sing, Benni, sing."

And so as Benni hauled the cake into the dining room, he sang.

"Hey, Blade," scowled the big man. "Did he call me Porky?"

"He did," replied Blade Boccelli. "Obviously he doesn't realize that my little brother don't appreciate that name."

"Little!" guffawed the four Gabriannis from across the table.

"I – I didn't mean no offence," stammered Benni.

"'Course you didn't," sneered Half-smile Gabrianni. "Besides, everybody calls Paul Boccelli 'Porky', don't they, Porky?"

52

"That's right, Porky," grinned the Weasel.

"It's not fair," said Porky. "Jimmy, you tell them!"

"Sure it's not fair," said One Finger Jimmy. "After all, he's about to share his cake around with everyone."

"I am?" gasped Porky. "But it's not much more than a muffin!"

"Some muffin," said Chainsaw Charlie. "Last time I saw a cake that size, the top flew open and three cops and a dog jumped out of it. It was the sneakiest ambush I ever fell for."

"Oh yeah?" sniggered the Weasel. "Pity Porky didn't get to the cake first. He'd have eaten them before they got out."

"That does it!" snapped Porky, suddenly whisking a massive knife from his sleeve.

In a blink, the four Gabrianni brothers had disappeared. Although they might laugh at the big man's size, they had the utmost respect for his skills with any form of eating utensil. One day you might hear the tale of when he took on the entire Eastside Fonetti gang armed only with a serviette and a teaspoon, but for the meantime we'll stick with the action in Luigi's.

"Where'd they go?" asked Porky, looking round.

One Finger Jimmy bent to peer under the table.

"Now ain't that cute!" he sneered. "Four little guys hugging the table legs."

"Come on out," said Porky. "I'm going to divide this cake up nice and fair between the seven of us."

The Gabriannis emerged sheepishly.

"It could be a trick!" whispered Numbers.

"No trick," said Porky. "I'll mark it out nice and fair, see what you think."

The large man very carefully traced lines through the icing, which divided the cake into seven long equal slices.

"There!" he said proudly. "Couldn't be fairer."

"Oh no?" sneered Half-smile. "So who gets the two end pieces with all the fancy icing?"

"Yeah, Porky," said Chainsaw, "and who gets the boring middle bits with hardly any icing at all?"

Luigi had been dreading something like this. It only took one small argument and suddenly his furniture

would become sawdust. If only
he had made the cake circular,
then it would have been easy
to divide it into seven
sections so that each one had
the same amount of icing! All
you need to do is find the
middle of the top and then mark
out seven pieces with equal angles....

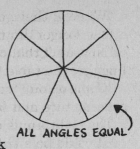

ALL ANGLES EQUAL

Luigi could have kicked himself. What on earth
had possessed him to make a *square* cake? It
seemed impossible to divide it so that each piece
would have the same amount of cake *and* have
exactly the same amount of icing ... but luckily for
Luigi, Murderous Maths has the answer!

TOP
BIT

SIDE
BIT

On a piece of cake there
are two bits of icing.
There's the bit on the top
and the bit down the
side.

Let's suppose you
measure right around
the four sides of the
cake and divide the
total distance round the
edge into seven equal
parts...

Suppose you then cut
from the very centre of

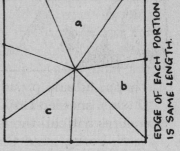

EDGE OF EACH PORTION
IS SAME LENGTH.

the cake out to each mark on the edge. Each piece of
icing at the side will be the same length, and so all
the side bits of icing will be equal.

The good bit is that each bit of icing on the top is also equal! This is because of triangles with the same area. Look at the pieces marked a and b. The "height" of each triangle is the distance from the edge of the cake to the middle. So long as the cake is square it doesn't matter which edge you measure from, so this means that both triangles have the same height. What's more, we've measured the pieces so that their bases are the same. If these triangles have the same height and the same base, that means the bits of cake underneath have the same area of icing on top and so there's the same amount of sponge underneath. Pieces a and b are exactly equal!

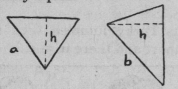

Now look at piece "c" and imagine it divided into two smaller triangles. Both triangles have the same height as piece a, so you can find out the total area of the two triangles by adding their bases together. When you do this, you get the same length of base as piece a. Therefore the two bits of piece c add up to the same area as piece a, so piece c is the same size as the others!

All the other pieces of the cake are also exactly the same size with the same amount of icing!

"Phew," said Luigi. "That bit of maths got us out of a murderous situation. Now we can relax."

Just then the door opened. In came a cloud of

perfume containing a lady carrying a fancy card-board box.

"Dolly Snowlips!" they all gasped, leaping to their feet.

"Relax, guys," drawled Dolly. "I just dropped by to wish my cuddlesome chum here many happy returns."

Her shoes clicked briskly across the floor towards Porky and she handed him the box.

"Th-thank you, ma'am," stuttered Porky, turning a deep crimson colour.

"What wouldn't I give for a lipstick in that shade," murmured Dolly as she gently stroked his cheek with a long fingernail. "Well, big boy, ain't ya gonna open your present?"

Everyone watched as Porky fumbled with the ribbon. The box came apart and there it was...

"What *is* it?" whispered Chainsaw as they all gawped at the blackened object inside.

"I baked it for you specially," said Dolly proudly.

"You? Baking? In a kitchen?" Blade burst out laughing then choked it back as Dolly shot him a glance that would have frozen the toes off a polar bear.

"And why not?" she snapped. "I figured if a loser like Luigi can cook, then anyone can do it. Besides, the only thing my old mammy ever left me was one of those hot cooking-machine what-d'ya-call-it jobs."

"An oven," they all said.

"Yeah, whatever," said Dolly. "So I figured it was time to give it a play. What do you think, then, big boy?"

"It's ... like a triangle," said Porky.

"I didn't have any fancy cake tin to cook it in, so I just borrowed the triangle from a pool table – you know, the one they use to set the balls up."

"I ain't never seen a cake that shape before," said Porky.

"You ain't never tasted a cake like that before," said Dolly. "It's my own recipe that I invented specially and it's all yours. Get those pretty cheeks around it, friend."

By now the smell from the cake had even overcome Dolly's perfume. All the others had backed away to the counter and were holding their noses.

"Go on, Porky!" laughed Weasel. "Take a nice big bite."

"And give it a good chew," chortled One Finger Jimmy.

"Don't forget to lick the plate when you've finished," added Charlie.

They couldn't stop smirking even when Porky produced his knife again.

"I couldn't do that!" said Porky.

"Couldn't do what?" asked Dolly crossly.

"Eat it all myself! No, I'm going to share this beautiful cake with my buddies here, if that's agreeable to you, ma'am."

The room went deathly silent.

"Why, that's a really kind gesture," said Dolly. "Step up, boys, and try a slice!"

"No no, really, we couldn't deprive you..." said Blade.

"Oh, I INSIST," said Porky. "Besides, you'd all like a chance to tell Dolly how much you appreciate her cooking, wouldn't you?"

The other six shuffled forward.

"I'd hate to think I was getting a bigger piece than anyone else," said Half-smile.

"Me too," said Blade. "You better divide that cake up nice and fair!"

"Oh no!" muttered Luigi, who was peering through the kitchen doorway. "Not again!"

Luckily for Luigi, the cake was in the shape of an equilateral triangle. All the sides were the same length and therefore the sides were all the same distance from the centre, just like the square. This is important because Porky could use the same method for dividing the cake up as he did before. All he needed to do was measure around the edge, divide by seven and then cut slices from the middle point.

When you work out the size of the pieces, you get lots of triangles with the same base and height just as with the square cake.

EDGE OF EACH PORTION IS SAME LENGTH.

Amazingly enough, this method works for any *regular polygon*. (You'll find out all about polygons in the next chapter.) This is just as well because…

60

See for yourself

Of course Murderous Maths fans don't automatically believe things they read in books, they like to get out there and SEE FOR THEMSELVES. That's why you're in the kitchen mixing up flour, eggs, water, butter, cream, lard, some green stuff you found in the bottom of a pot that you want to use up, margarine and milk to make a cake to experiment on. Slap it in the microwave for a couple of hours on full blast, then out it comes: a perfect square sponge cake. It's still plain of course (well it's plain black actually – probably a fault with the microwave) so you reach into the cupboard for something to coat it with. All you can find is a large jar of fish paste, so you prise open the top and suddenly...

"Har har!" comes a voice. "Didn't expect me, did you?"

Your archenemy Professor Fiendish leaps out of the jar and cackles triumphantly. "I knew you'd fall into my trap sooner or later."

"Exactly how long have you been hiding in there?" you ask in amazement as you stare at him. His entire body is glistening with fishy oil and he's scooping pink goo out from inside his shirt.

"I wasn't hiding," he snarls. "OK, I had an unfortunate dispute with a tuna fish about who was higher in the food chain, but that's not important right now. The fact is I'm out, and unless you solve my diabolical cake challenge, you'll be taking my place in the jar."

You try to look unconcerned but he stinks. He *really* stinks. And normally a bit of fish paste would smell rather appetizing, but to be shoved headfirst into an entire pot of the stuff does not seem appealing, especially as *he's* been in there for weeks without a shower. Or a toilet for that matter.

"You have to divide that square cake up into eight absolutely equal pieces," he says.

"Is that it?" you reply. "That's not exactly very diabolical."

"Har har," he snarls. "The diabolical bit is that you are only allowed THREE straight cuts with the knife."

"Still easy," you say. Quickly you chop the cake into quarters, then put the bits on top of each other. One more slice through all four pieces will make eight pieces altogether...

← 1ST CUT

2ND CUT

← 3RD CUT GOES THROUGH ALL FOUR PIECES.

"NO!" he screams. "You've got to make eight equal bits with three cuts and NO MOVING THE CAKE AROUND. Now *that's* diabolical!"

Quick! Before the smell of rancid fish paste overcomes you, can you solve the Professor's challenge?

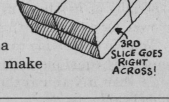

Answer:
Use your first two cuts to slice the cake into quarters. The third cut goes through the cake horizontally, slicing it into a top layer and a bottom layer. This will make eight identical pieces.

3RD SLICE GOES RIGHT ACROSS!

So do triangle angles always add up to 180°?

Have a think about this fine old mind-bender:

- A hunter decides to go bear hunting so he sets out from his base camp and walks one kilometre south where he sees a bear. He smirks as he loads his gun. This is going to be *so* easy.

HEE HEE!

- The bear grabs the gun, bites it in two and spits the bits back at him.

PTOO!

YIKES!

- The hunter breaks the world land speed record as he runs away one kilometre east.

- He then walks one kilometre north and arrives back at his base camp where he changes into some clean underwear.

- So what colour was the bear?

Isn't that a beauty?

There are two strange things about this puzzle. The obvious one is: how can you possibly work out what colour the bear was? The other point is: how could the explorer get back home again? If he walks one kilometre south, one kilometre east and then one kilometre north, you'd think he'd end up a kilometre away from his base.

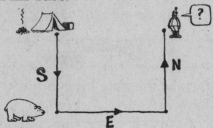

In fact there is one place on the Earth where this journey would be possible!

Suppose the explorer's base was at the *North Pole*. First he walks a kilometre south, but then when he runs a kilometre east, this would just take him around in a little arc (of radius 1 kilometre) around the North Pole. Finally he just needs to walk a kilometre north to bring him back to the North Pole again!

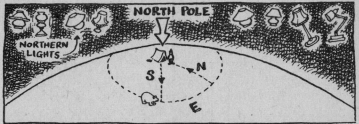

Therefore, the bear must be a polar bear – so it's white!

The interesting bit is that he's walked in three straight lines which all join up so it's a triangle, but the three angles are all 90° making 270° altogether. That's a lot more than the 180° we'd normally expect for a triangle. The scary thing is that if you start drawing triangles on spheres rather than flat paper, the angles can add up to anything between 180° and 540°.

Wouldn't it be lovely to know all about the properties of triangles on curved surfaces? Of course it would but unfortunately the triangles chapter should have finished about ten pages ago, so we'll have to leave it. Now isn't that a pity?

POLYGONS

Any shape with straight sides is called a polygon.

Good grief, this book has fallen into the hands of hecklers! All right then, let's try again:

Any shape with straight sides is called a polygon unless it only has one side.

Now you're being silly. You can't have a shape with two straight sides.

Right! That does it. We'll do demonstrations of polygons instead and we'll start with different hexagons. The "hex" bit means the shape has to have six straight sides, and if it's *regular* that means all the sides and angles have to be the same. The other three hexagons are *irregular*. You might notice that these hexagons also have bumps in the middle, but mathematically speaking this isn't strictly necessary.

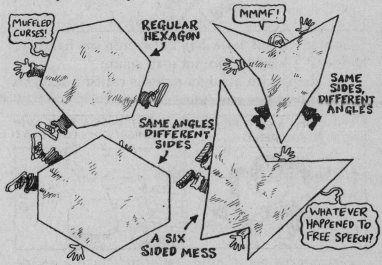

You can always tell how many sides a polygon has by the first bit of the name (which comes from the Greek or Latin words for different numbers):

PENT-agon = 5 sides

HEX-agon = 6 sides

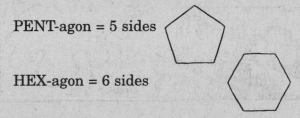

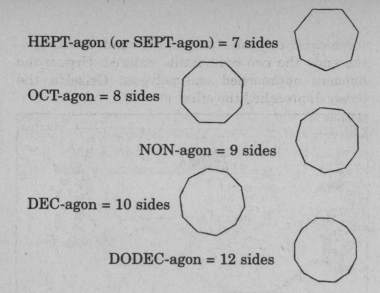

HEPT-agon (or SEPT-agon) = 7 sides

OCT-agon = 8 sides

NON-agon = 9 sides

DEC-agon = 10 sides

DODEC-agon = 12 sides

These can all be either regular or irregular. Of course there are also...

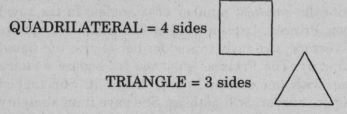

QUADRILATERAL = 4 sides

TRIANGLE = 3 sides

The various possible names get a bit more complicated here, but all we need to know for now is that a regular quadrilateral is better known as a SQUARE and the regular triangle is an EQUILATERAL triangle.

Chopping polygons into triangles
The sun beat down on the hushed arena. The expectant crowd gazed in awe at the two identical

seven-sided polygons lying in the sand. From oppo-
site ends the two combatants entered. Urgum the
Axeman approached one polygon, Grizelda the
Grisly approached the other.

They eyed each other warily. They raised their
weapons. The contest? Who could chop their polygon
into the *smallest* number of triangles. In the royal
box, Princess Laplace held up the gilded set square.
Everyone anxiously waited for her to give the signal
to start. The Princess gave the set square a sharp
tap with her eraser. Nobody heard it. She tapped
again, harder. Still nothing. She gave it an almighty
clout, but the fact is that when you tap a set square
with a rubber, the noise doesn't carry across a giant
stadium full of people.

"Oh, for goodness' sake!" she yelled. "JUST GET
ON WITH IT!"

And so the duel commenced.

Apart from the starting signal, the Princess had
been rather clever. Urgum had been threatening an
all-out war following his discovery that Grizelda's
cat had been using his window box. Grizelda had

denied it, but the trouble with barbarians is that they never know quite when to back down. If the Princess hadn't suggested this challenge, the sands of the Forgotten Desert would soon have been dripping in gore. As it was, the winner of the contest was claiming the other's head as a prize, but the Princess hoped that this could be avoided.

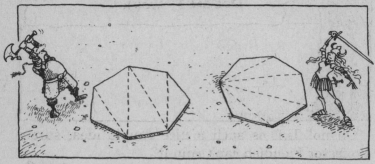

To chop a polygon into the *smallest* number of triangles, always chop it from corner to corner. Here you can see how Urgum and Grizelda plan to chop their polygons, but even though their ways are different, they both produce the same number of triangles. The Princess had fixed a contest where the only losers would be the circling vultures. Phew!

You can divide any polygon up into triangles, and the smallest number is always two fewer than the number of sides the polygon has. So for a seven-sided polygon, you'll always get five triangles. A nine-sided polygon will give seven triangles and so on.

This is handy for working out what all the angles of a polygon add up to. As each triangle has 180°, you must multiply 180° by the number of triangles. Here's how it goes:

70

NUMBER OF SIDES	NUMBER OF TRIANGLES	TOTAL OF ANGLES
4	2	$180 \times 2 = 360°$
5	3	$180 \times 3 = 540°$
6	4	$180 \times 4 = 720°$
7	5	$180 \times 5 = 900°$

RUBBISH! I CAN SHOW THIS DOESN'T WORK!

Oh no! This is such a nice simple idea, surely Professor Fiendish can't ruin it?

HAR HAR! IT'S GOT SIX SIDES, BUT I'VE SPLIT IT INTO TWO TRIANGLES!

Good grief, he's right even if he does still smell a bit fishy. The trouble is that each shape has four corners, but the angle at one corner is 180°.

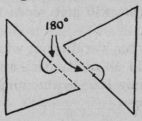

180°

This is confusing stuff, so we'll have to avoid it happening with an extra rule: *You can't make any cuts that are directly in line with an edge.* Now let's see what we get...

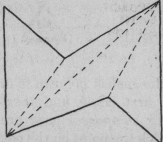

That's better! Now you can chop up any straight-sided shape, although be warned that some shapes are more savage than others...

How to draw regular polygons

You can draw a regular polygon with any number of sides, but some are a lot easier than others. There are lots of different ways of drawing them, but one good way is to start by drawing a circle to fit your polygon inside. Mark the middle with a tiny cross and then decide what sort of polygon takes your fancy.

Easyness guide:

 PUSSYCAT BEWARE

 APPROACH WITH CAUTION HAVE BANDAGES READY

HEXAGON

This is much the easiest polygon to draw:

1 Draw your first circle and then, KYCOETSD (*keeping your compasses open exactly the same distance*), stick the point on the edge of the circle. Draw two little arcs that cut the circle.

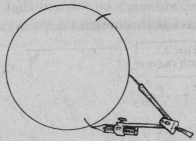

2 Stick the compasses point in where one of the arcs cuts the circle and draw another arc further round the circle. Then move your compasses to the new arc and draw another arc, and so on until you've got six arcs marked around the circle.

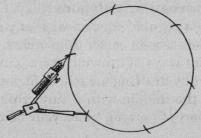

3 Join up the six arcs.

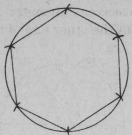

TRIANGLE (EQUILATERAL)

Follow exactly the same instructions for the hexagon, but only join up every second arc. As this is far too easy for any Murderous Maths reader, to make it a bit more exciting you have to do it BLINDFOLDED. Have a cloth handy to wipe up the blood when you shove the compass point through your finger.

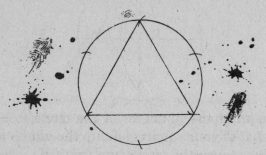

SQUARE

There are two ways to do a square which depend on whether you want to choose the length of the diagonals or the length of the sides. Both methods start like this:

1 Draw your circle, then draw a diameter right across the middle.

2 Open your compasses slightly more and then stick

them in where the diameter hits one side. Draw
an arc that crosses the diameter. KYCOETSD and
stick them in at the other end of the diameter and
draw another arc.

3 Draw a line through both places where the arcs
cross, long enough so it crosses the circle.

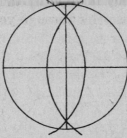

4 If you want the diameter of the circle to be the
diagonal of your square: join up the places where
the lines touch the circle, and that's it.

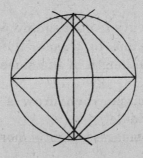

5 If you want the radius of your circle to be the *side* of a square, reset your compasses to the radius of the circle and look at this:

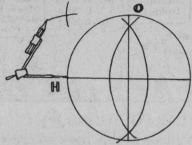

6 Stick your compasses in at H (for Here) and draw an arc roughly where the fourth corner of the square will be. KYCOETSD and stick them in at O (for Over there) and do the same.

7 Join H and O to the place where the arcs cross and there's your square. Then if you want to be sneaky, rub out all the rest of the big circle and *nobody will ever know how you did it*.

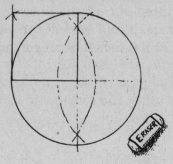

8 Throw a party for loads of showbiz personalities to celebrate your new square. You'd be amazed at how many of them will turn up, and gush on about what a fabulous square it is and how they've always been big fans of yours. The fact is they'll do anything if they think they'll get their photo taken.

OTHER REGULAR POLYGONS

This is the only place in this book where you *might* have to do some sums, because you need to divide some simple numbers to find the angles you need. (You might be interested to know that the very fussiest of the Ancient Greeks refused to do anything as naff as measuring angles and dividing them. As a result there were lots of polygon shapes they couldn't draw.) However, ages ago we did promise that this book would be a NO SUMS zone, so we've printed out all the answers ready for you. Don't thank us, it's all part of the job.

Let's look at a finished heptagon and then see how it got there:

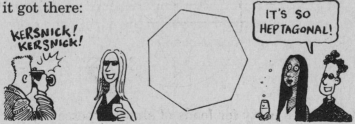

As you can see, the seven points of the heptagon all lie on a circle, so to start with you need to draw a circle the same size as you want your finished shape to be. Mark the centre with a little cross and then draw in one radius (i.e. a line from the centre to the outside).

If you look at the finished drawing you'll see a heptagon needs seven lines coming from the centre of the circle. These are the next bits we need to do, and here's where the dividing sum comes in. We need to get the same angle between each of these lines, so as there are 360° in a full circle, we need to divide this into 7 equal bits. The sum is $360 \div 7 = 51°$. (Actually it's 51·428571° but that's impossible to draw unless you have a surgical laser and piece of paper the size of Australia. If you manage to draw an angle of about 51° accurately then you're doing fine.)

So grab your protractor and measure an angle of 51° and draw another radius to the edge. Then draw another, and another and so on...

HINT: when you get to the last line, don't measure the angle. Just put your line exactly in the middle of the gap – so if your angles haven't been absolutely exact, this will help even things out.

Finally join up the seven places where the lines touch the circle, and there's your heptagon!

The angle between the radii in the middle is called the "central angle" and, as we've seen, for a heptagon it's about 51°. To save you dividing, here are the central angles for different polygons:

SHAPE	CENTRAL ANGLE
TRIANGLE	120°
SQUARE	90°
PENTAGON	72°
HEXAGON	60°
HEPTAGON	ABOUT 51°
OCTAGON	45°
NONAGON	40°
DECAGON	36°
TRICENTIHEXADECAGON	1°
MILLAGON	0.36°
GOOGLAGON	0.0000000000000000000000000 0000000000000000000000000 0000000000000 0000000000000 0000000000000000000000000 036°

Note: the googlagon is in the ⚠ category because the sun will have expanded to a red giant and consumed the Earth in a nuclear inferno before you finish drawing it.

Regular polygon facts

If you've just made up your own heptagon, you might have realized a few things about regular polygons:

● You can always draw a circle that touches all the corners.

● You can always draw a circle that touches the middles of all the sides.

● They have as many lines of reflectional symmetry as they have sides. (This means you can fold them down any of the dotted lines and the two halves will overlap exactly.)

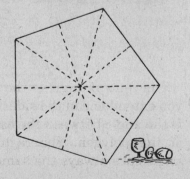

- They have as many positions of rotational symmetry as they have sides. ("Rotational symmetry" means you can spin them round and you won't know which way up they started.)

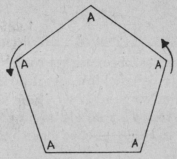

- All the central angles are equal. (For instance, we worked out that all the angles in the middle of the heptagon are 51·428571°. If they weren't equal then it wouldn't be a regular polygon.)
- The external angle is equal to the central angle.

This one involves the original rules of geometry, but it's rather neat. Look at this:

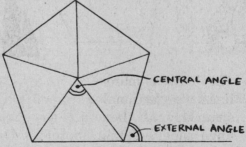

CENTRAL ANGLE

EXTERNAL ANGLE

The central angle is the one in the middle, and if you extend one of the sides a bit, the **external** angle is the angle between the extension and the next side of the polygon. For regular polygons, these two angles are always the same.

This is rather cool, because we can show that this ALWAYS has to be true! We just need to remember three things that we've learnt:

1 All three angles in a triangle add up to 180°.
2 An isosceles triangle has two sides and two angles the same.
3 Congruent triangles are exactly the same as each other.

If we draw a circle round the polygon, it becomes clear...

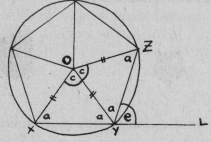

First have a look at the triangle OXY. As the sides OX and OY are both radii of the circle they have to be the same length. Therefore the triangle is isosceles, and that means the angles marked "a" are equal.

Triangle OYZ is exactly the same shape and size as OXY (in other words it's "congruent") because the sides are the same lengths and both the central angles c have to be equal. This means that all the angles marked "a" in both triangles are the same.

Finally, we know the angles in a triangle make 180° so in triangle XOY we can see that a + a + c = 180° We also know that the angles on a straight line must make 180° so if you look at the extended line XL: a + a + e = 180°

If a + a + c = 180° and a + a + e = 180° then c must equal e.

Therefore the central angle is equal to the exterior angle, and this is true for any regular polygon, even if it has 329 sides.

That was a bit like hard work, so here's a nice cute thing about regular polygons to finish with:

● You can always make neat star patterns with them. Just extend each line so that it joins up with another like this:

 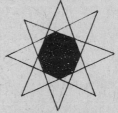

If you want to make your stars spikier, here's one idea...

1 Start by making a polygon in the same way we did the heptagon earlier. Put little crosses where the radii touch the lines, but don't join them up yet.

2 Draw a bigger circle outside the first circle. Extend the radii so that they touch the *opposite* side of the big circle. (The diagram shows you what to do.) Mark little crosses where they meet.

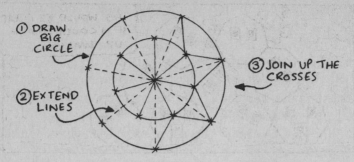

3 Join up the crosses to make a star pattern! You can then rub out all the other marks and just leave a perfect star. The bigger you make your second circle, the spikier your star will be.

Generally polygons are rather fun, but there's just one thing about polygons which is truly awful. Brace yourself because here it comes:

Isn't that dreadful? Don't say we didn't warn you.

Shoving shapes together

People nearly always build houses and flats with right-angled corners because they fit together neatly. Of course you could build a street full of regular heptagonal houses, but it would look a bit odd. A block of heptagonal flats would look even odder!

You can see this would lead to all sorts of problems, one of the biggest being all the wasted space between the flats. That's why we usually stick to squares and rectangles when we're building.

Using good old right angles everywhere also has the extra advantage of giving us horizontal floors and vertical walls. However, there's also a disadvantage: we're wasting space! Using exactly the same amount of building materials we could make a bigger block of flats, providing nobody minded living in...

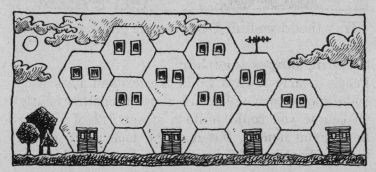

85

…hexagons! Hexagons all fit together neatly, and they are bigger inside. (If you draw a square which measures 60m round the outside, the area is 225 square metres. But a hexagon that measures 60m round the outside has an area of almost 260 square metres.)

Of course we hardly ever build with hexagons, but that's because we're not as clever as BEES. A honeycomb is a massive array of hexagons because bees have worked out that they get the most space by using them. In terms of efficient architecture then, the score is: Bees 1 Humans 0.

Strange buildings and alien humour

One of the most famous buildings in the world is named after its own very peculiar shape, and following a special Murderous Maths investigation we can now reveal the REAL reason why the American defence headquarters is based in a huge building called "The Pentagon".

Let's suppose the building was "The Hexagon". It wouldn't be long before some evil intelligence from outside the galaxy took advantage…

Of course, Americans are pretty clever and thought something like this could happen. That's why they chose a shape that wouldn't fit together with itself.

Incidentally, this information is strictly classified, so if you happen to be on a bus with the management committee of the Pentagon and you ask them about this, you can be sure they will just try to laugh and pretend you're wrong. But *you'll* know it's the truth, and *they'll know that you know,* but most importantly *you'll know that they know that you know* and what really bothers them is that *even if they know that you know that they know that you know*, they can't do a thing about it.

Complete cover

When a shape will completely cover a surface without gaps, you say it will **tessellate**. This leads to some rather satisfying little experiments, as you'll see. Of the regular polygons you can only use triangles, squares and hexagons.

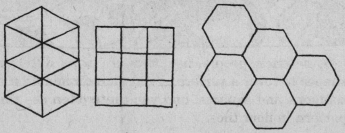

For irregular shapes you can use any triangle or quadrilateral. Otherwise you can experiment making your own shapes with five sides or more.

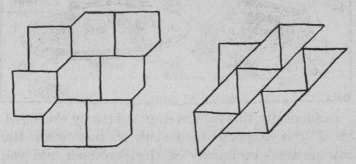

The artist MC Escher was brilliant at inventing shapes like this – here's a detail from one of his pictures which might inspire you to have a go:

Sometimes people use two or more different shapes to cover a surface. A common combination is octagons and squares, and you quite often see this pattern in floor tiles.

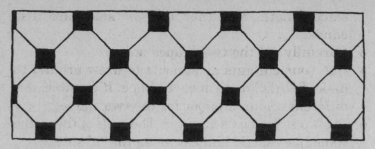

There's just one thing about all these patterns though – they repeat themselves. It's a bit like fancy wallpaper, if you look along it you'll see that the same pattern keeps coming back. Nothing wrong in that, but if you want to try something that's quite bizarre, you'll need to make some...

Penrose tiles

These amazing tiles are just one of the fabulous maths things invented by Roger Penrose. If you're a true Murderous Maths fan, remember that name because our Mr Penrose has come up with some of the grooviest stuff in maths.

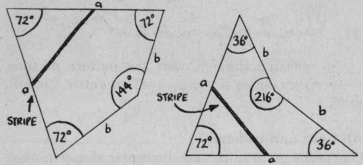

- Draw out these two shapes on to some nice thick card. Try to get the angles as accurate as possible, and make sure the "a" sides are all the

90

same length, and that the "b" sides are also equal.

- Carefully cut the two shapes out.
- Use your cut-outs as stencils to draw around to make LOADS more of each shape. If possible, use different coloured paper for the two shapes.
- Draw a stripe on each shape. The ends of the stripe should be exactly halfway along the "a" sides.

You now have to put your tiles together and try to cover as big an area as possible without any gaps. There's just one rule, the stripes must join up.

The amazing thing is that the pattern of tiles *never repeats* even if you covered an entire football pitch!

All bent and twisted

One of the great things about regular shapes is that it doesn't matter where in the universe you go, a square is always pretty much the same thing. So is a regular triangle, pentagon, hexagon or googlagon for that matter. Therefore, if you can show that you're familiar with them, your high intelligence will be respected by any three-dimensional life-form anywhere. Even in a restaurant on the distant planet Jannf...

As it happens, your quick wit and easy charm recently came to the attention of the Earth's Defence Federation, and that's why you now find yourself sitting in the most sumptuous eating emporium in the universe. Unfortunately, sitting opposite you is the leader of the Evil Gollarks from the planet Zog. Your mission is to seek a diplomatic solution to stop all their futile invasion attempts, so it's no wonder that you're desperate not to make a complete nana of yourself.

The sniffy waitress glides up to take your order. Of course, as it's the most sumptuous place in the universe, there's no menu and you can have absolutely anything you like. You do your best to impress.

Ooops. She'll go back and tell all her mates in the kitchen, and then word will get out that Earthlings are just too pathetic to live. You sadly reach for your paper serviette...

Hang on! That's no good. No good at all. As the whole universe knows, in any civilized society a serviette should be a perfect square. Maybe the food on Jannf isn't what you expected, but at least you can show them something that they'll understand and respect. You pull out a pencil to draw a square...

The situation is getting out of hand. Somehow you MUST show them that a serviette should be square, but what do you do?

The answer is *origami*, but don't tell them that. On the planet Jannf, "origami" means "the gas from your socks would blot out a supernova" and you'd probably end up on a plate yourself. However, as far as we're concerned, "origami" means paper folding and it's a rather neat thing to be able to do.

You need to fold the serviette into an exact square shape and by so doing you'll bring culture and enlightenment to the furthest corners of the universe. Here's how to fold a perfect square from any piece of paper:

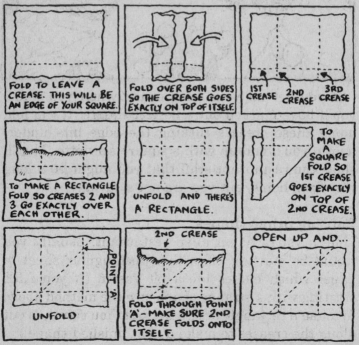

FOLD TO LEAVE A CREASE. THIS WILL BE AN EDGE OF YOUR SQUARE.

FOLD OVER BOTH SIDES SO THE CREASE GOES EXACTLY ON TOP OF ITSELF.

1ST CREASE   2ND CREASE   3RD CREASE

TO MAKE A RECTANGLE FOLD SO CREASES 2 AND 3 GO EXACTLY OVER EACH OTHER.

UNFOLD AND THERE'S A RECTANGLE.

TO MAKE A SQUARE FOLD SO 1ST CREASE GOES EXACTLY ON TOP OF 2ND CREASE.

POINT 'A'

UNFOLD

2ND CREASE

FOLD THROUGH POINT 'A' - MAKE SURE 2ND CREASE FOLDS ONTO ITSELF.

OPEN UP AND...

94

If you get all your folds exact, when you finish you'll have marked out a perfect square. If you fold along these creases tucking the edge bits underneath, you'll end up with a square serviette. That'll show the restaurant staff that you might be a long way from home, but you are not a savage.

Folding other shapes

Unless you're at an alien restaurant, usually you would be starting off with a rectangular sheet of paper which makes life a bit easier. (If you ARE starting with a strange shape, use the method above to make a rectangle or square first. You can then cut along the creases to make a neat finished shape.)

Get some paper and try these for a bit of fun:

SQUARE

If you start with a rectangle, here's the foolproof way to make the biggest possible square out of it:

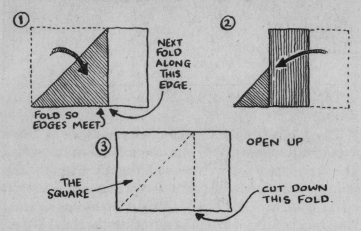

① FOLD SO EDGES MEET. NEXT FOLD ALONG THIS EDGE.

②

③ THE SQUARE. OPEN UP. CUT DOWN THIS FOLD.

EQUILATERAL TRIANGLE

Start with a rectangular piece of paper...

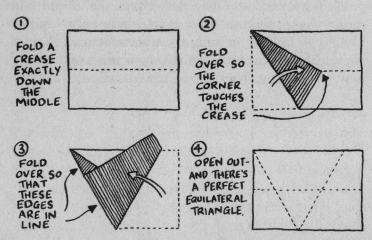

① FOLD A CREASE EXACTLY DOWN THE MIDDLE

② FOLD OVER SO THE CORNER TOUCHES THE CREASE

③ FOLD OVER SO THAT THESE EDGES ARE IN LINE

④ OPEN OUT AND THERE'S A PERFECT EQUILATERAL TRIANGLE.

HEXAGON

If you've made an equilateral triangle, it's easy to convert it into a perfect hexagon.

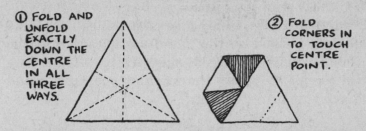

① FOLD AND UNFOLD EXACTLY DOWN THE CENTRE IN ALL THREE WAYS.

② FOLD CORNERS IN TO TOUCH CENTRE POINT.

PENTAGON

You might think it would be hard to fold a perfect pentagon, what with the angles all having to be 108° and so on, but here are *two* ways to do it, and we aren't charging you extra.

The POSH way, starting with a square:

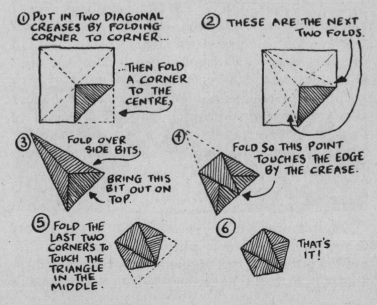

① PUT IN TWO DIAGONAL CREASES BY FOLDING CORNER TO CORNER...

...THEN FOLD A CORNER TO THE CENTRE.

② THESE ARE THE NEXT TWO FOLDS.

③ FOLD OVER SIDE BITS.

BRING THIS BIT OUT ON TOP.

④ FOLD SO THIS POINT TOUCHES THE EDGE BY THE CREASE.

⑤ FOLD THE LAST TWO CORNERS TO TOUCH THE TRIANGLE IN THE MIDDLE.

⑥ THAT'S IT!

This is the method to use if your pentagon is likely to be going on display in a museum. However, if you're in a mad rush, you should try doing it the FUMBLY way. Here's how...

Since you first folded a square, things have gone so well for you at the Jannf restaurant that the Gollark even felt obliged to pay the bill. As the long till receipt flies from the machine you grab it and quickly tie it into a knot...

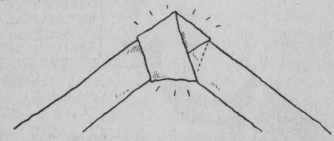

Yes, this does work! It must be one of the oddest things in maths, but to make a pentagon you just need to get a long rectangular strip of paper and tie a knot in it. If you do it very carefully and feed the bit of paper through itself as far as you can before you get any creases in it, you should finally be able to squash it flat into a pentagon shape. (This works especially well if you tie a knot in a drinking straw squashed flat.)

Origami is great fun, and when you get the hang of it you can go on to make all sorts of amazing shapes and models. Imagine...

LEADERSHIP OF THE UNIVERSE IS YOURS, OH BRILLIANT ONE!

To start with, though, why not try some realistic animal models like these:

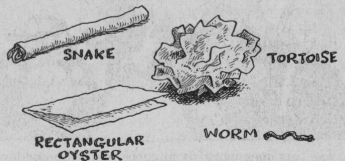

SNAKE

TORTOISE

RECTANGULAR OYSTER

WORM

There are lots of good books about origami, and you can also find links to some great origami websites on *www.murderousmaths.co.uk*.

VICIOUS CIRCLES

There are hundreds of strange things that turn up when you're just doodling a few lines and circles. Here are four of the simpler tricks to try, but if you haven't got a pair of compasses handy, don't worry! You don't need to know where the centre of the circle is for any of these tricks, so you can just draw circles around coins or mugs or a bicycle wheel or anything else that's round.

HOLD STILL, CAN'T YOU?

Circle trick one
- Draw a big circle to fill the page.
- Mark six points anywhere around the circumference.
- Go round these points labelling them in order A, B, C, c, b, a. (Notice that A and a are neighbours and so are C and c.)
- You now need to draw a straight line by joining up points A and b. Then draw a second straight line joining points B and a. Mark the place where they cross with a little "x"
- Draw two more straight lines joining A to c and then C to a. Mark where they cross with an "x"

- Finally draw two straight lines joining B to c and then C to b and again mark where they cross with an "x".
- Here's the strange bit. It doesn't matter where on the circle you put the six points to start with, you'll find that the three crossing points marked "x" are ALWAYS in a straight line!

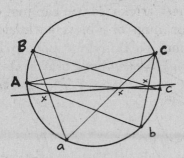

Circle trick two

- Draw a medium-sized circle.
- You need to draw six "tangents" that touch the circle. A tangent is a line that touches the side of the circle but doesn't go inside. These six tangents can touch the circle anywhere, so long as they all link up on the outside of the circle. Have a look at Mr Reeve's picture on the next page to get the idea.
- There should be six places where each tangent crosses its neighbours. Go round these crossing places and number them 1, 2, 3, 1, 2, 3.
- Draw a straight line joining points 1 to 1. Do another joining 2 to 2 and a third joining 3 to 3.
- If you've done it carefully, these last three lines should all cross each other at the same place!

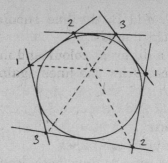

Later in the book we'll find out how to draw ellipses – and amazingly both these tricks also work with ellipses. (You need to be VERY good at drawing though!)

Circle trick three

- Draw three circles that cross over each other at a common point. (Look at the point marked C in the diagram.) Your circles can be different sizes.
- Mark three tiny crosses at the other places where the circles cut each other.
- Choose one circle and call it Daisy. Mark a tiny cross anywhere on the outside edge. We've called it D for Daisy here.
- Draw lines from D through the two crosses on Daisy. Mark where they hit the other circles A and B.

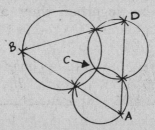

- If you join A and B, the line should always go through the third cross!
- Why not use a different colour and mark "D" in a different place. Draw the lines again – it should still work!

Circle trick four
- Draw a large circle on paper.
- Put four little crosses *anywhere* around the edge of the circle.
- Join up the crosses to make a quadrilateral. (Because all the corners touch the circle, this is called a **cyclic quadrilateral**.) Shade one pair of opposite corners.

- Cut out the quadrilateral, and tear off the corners.
- If you put together the two shaded corners, they make a straight line! And if you put the unshaded corners together they also make a straight line.

There's a rule to describe this last trick: *The opposite angles of a cyclic quadrilateral always add up to 180°.*

As 180° is a straight line, according to this rule the opposite corners put together should always make a straight line.

Bah! The trouble with maths is that if you say something *always* does something, somebody somewhere is bound to ask you why. Luckily this one isn't too difficult to prove. All you need to know are what isosceles triangles are and that the radii of circles are always the same length.

Here's a cyclic quadrilateral, and to show why the rule works, we draw in the centre point and then draw lines out to each of the four corners.

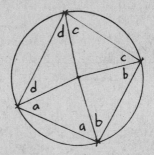

Because all the lines from the centre are equal lengths, we end up with four isosceles triangles.

Each triangle has two equal angles, and here the equal angles are marked a,a b,b c,c and d,d.

Suppose you cut out the quadrilateral and put all four angles together. They would make 360°.

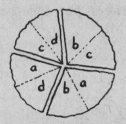

What's more you would find that there were *two* each of angles a,b,c and d. Now suppose you only had *one* each of a,b,c, and d – that would only make 180° which is a straight line.

Look at the diagram and pick two opposite angles. You'll see between them they have one each of a,b,c and d. Therefore if you pick two opposite angles, they must add up to 180°. We've proved it!

OK, it's not exactly rock and roll, but be honest – it's quietly satisfying, isn't it?

The Fastbuck Gazette

TINNED TONGUE TERROR

Fastbuck's tinned tongue factory could become a victim of its own success. Recently they have been working flat out to meet the surge in demand for tinned tongue. When asked why the product was so popular, the director Mr Dan White replied: "Our tinned tongues speak for themselves." But the giant circular tank that holds all the rejects and off-cuts from the factory is about to overflow. If nothing is done, then the whole city could be engulfed in a tide of tongues. When asked to comment, Mr White was tongue-tied.

Once again, another gross news story from the foul city of Fastbuck! Further investigation reveals that the tank does have an emergency drain, but in typical Fastbuck fashion, the handle to open it is situated right in the middle of the tank. The only way to reach the handle is to lie a ladder across the edges of the tank and crawl to it but...

...the ladder isn't quite long enough to get across the centre of the tank. (You can't lean the ladder on the handle.) The nearest you can get to the handle is by crawling to the middle of the ladder and stretching over, but the handle is just out of reach. (By the way, don't look down because some of the tongues in there are still twitching. We don't call these books "Murderous Maths" for nothing you know.)

Is it worth trying to move the ladder round the circle to get closer to the handle?

The answer is NO, and to understand why, we'll find out a bit about **chords**.

HERE ARE SOME NICE CHORDS TO SERENADE VERONICA WITH.

STRUM CHUNNG VUSHUNG

AND IN RETURN I'LL MARINATE PONGO.

GLOOSH! FRAZZZZAP! AAAARGH!

Er, no, we're not talking about that sort of chord. The sort of chord we're talking about is a straight line drawn across a circle.

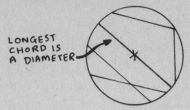

You'll notice that the longest chord you can draw goes through the centre of the circle – and so of course it's the same thing as the diameter of the circle. There's one fairly obvious thing to know about chords: *Chords of the same length are the same distance from the centre of the circle.*

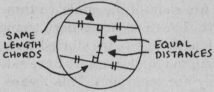

Here we have two chords that are the same length. To get the distance of a chord from the centre, you simply draw a line from the centre to exactly halfway along the chord. (It's like dropping a perpendicular, just as we saw with the Colonel on the beach on page 26). If you measure them, you'll find that these two chords are the same distance from the centre.

No problem! All we need is a circle with two equal chords, and we join the ends to the centre. What do we get...

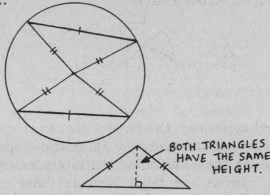

BOTH TRIANGLES HAVE THE SAME HEIGHT.

...two congruent triangles. Each triangle has two sides that are radii of the circle, so they are all the same length. The third side of each triangle is one of the same length chords we started with, so they're the same length too. If triangles have sides the same length, they are congruent. This means they must have the same height, and this height is the distance of the chord to the centre of the circle.

How satisfying, but in case you'd forgotten, you're still dangling over the Fastbuck tongue tank. It doesn't matter where you put the ladder, you'll always be just out of reach of the handle. One slip and you'll fall in and be licked to a dribbly death.

By the way, suppose you've got two ladders which are both slightly too short to reach straight across the tank. Can you use a bit of Murderous Maths thinking to see how would you reach the handle? (And it isn't safe to tie the two ladders together to make one long ladder!)

Answer:

Chords and cameras

Here's something else strange about chords. Imagine you're in a huge circular room, and somebody has put an absolutely massive portrait of you against the wall. Gorgeous, eh? You stand with your back to the wall on the other side of the room and hold up your camera, which does not have anything fancy like a zoom or wide-angle lens. You discover that when you look through the camera, the portrait is exactly the right width to fit the viewfinder. The odd thing is that it doesn't matter where on the wall you stand, you still find that the portrait exactly fits!

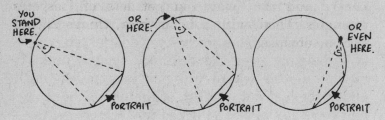

A camera with a fixed lens always has the same angle of vision which you can see in the diagram marked as C. The odd bit is that if you have a chord and draw two lines to *any* place on the edge of the circle, the angle the lines meet at will always be the same.

PROVE IT!

OK, OK, keep your wig on! He'll have to wait a minute, because we're going to look at something else first. In maths speak you can say: *the angle at the centre is twice the angle at the edge*. The diagram shows what we mean.

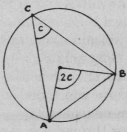

Amazingly enough, if you keep a clear head and take things one step at a time, you can prove that this ALWAYS has to be true! The great secret of proving circle things is to join everything to the centre and that way you get lots of isosceles triangles. Then, with a bit of luck, things should become obvious.

Let's see what we've got. Because the radii of a circle are always equal, we've ended up with three isosceles triangles and the equal angles are marked xx, yy and zz. Our chord is the line AB, so what we need to prove is that the angle in the middle marked q is twice as big as the angle at C. You'll see that the diagram has split C into two angles z and y, so we can say $C = z + y$. As q is supposed to be twice as big as C, what we need to show is that $q = 2z + 2y$. Fasten your seat belts – here we go:

- As the angles in a triangle add up to 180°, you know that in the triangle AOB $q + x + x = 180°$. (We can write this as $q + 2x = 180°$).
- In the big triangle ABC, the angles must also add up to 180° and if you count up all the little bits you get $2x + 2y + 2z = 180°$.
- As $q + 2x$ and $2x + 2y + 2z$ both add up to 180°, we know they must be the same, so we can put this: $q + 2x = 2x + 2y + 2z$.
- Finally, if you know the first thing about equations, you'll know that because there's a 2x on both sides, we can remove them. And when we take them away we're left with... $q = 2y + 2z$. We've done it!

OH! HAVE YOU?

The good bit is that we didn't say whereabouts on the circle "C" had to be. It always works so long as "C" stays on the same side of the chord. In fact, we can show that this even works when "C" is pushed right over like this...

...shhhh! He's dozed off, so let's skip the proof and take a chance to deal with something we saw right back on page 12.

Imagine a circle drawn with a diameter across it and an angle at the edge like this:

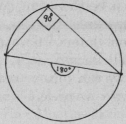

As we just saw, the angle at the centre is twice the angle at the edge – BUT as the diameter is a straight line the angle at the centre is 180°. So the angle at the edge must be half 180° which is 90°. As Thales said, "The angle in a semicircle is a right angle."

Now it's a time for a bit of a treat: the Murderous Maths Organization is absolutely thrilled to announce that we've got a very special guest who has kindly agreed to present our final item about circles. So please put your hands together and welcome our very own top TV celebrity and game show host as...

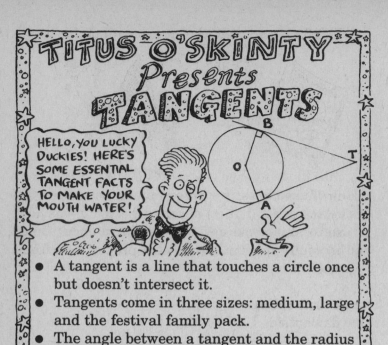

TITUS "O'SKINTY" Presents TANGENTS

HELLO, YOU LUCKY DUCKIES! HERE'S SOME ESSENTIAL TANGENT FACTS TO MAKE YOUR MOUTH WATER!

- A tangent is a line that touches a circle once but doesn't intersect it.
- Tangents come in three sizes: medium, large and the festival family pack.
- The angle between a tangent and the radius at the point of contact is always 90°.
- Tangents have smooth creamy centres encased in chunky chocolate.
- From any external point, two tangents can be drawn to a circle. These tangents will always be equal in length.
- There are loads of exciting Tangent flavours including orange ripple, coffee delight, lemon crush, salty mushroom and toothpaste.
- So next time you want to show someone how much you love them, treat them to a Tangent.
- Tangents are available from Skinty stores.

114

STOP! That's enough. Go on ... get out of this book!

Huh. To be honest we were a bit surprised that he agreed to appear, but we never suspected it was just a ruse to plug some naff sweets. Sorry about that, but hopefully you can sort out the proper facts from the rubbish.

Rock and rollers
One day outside Udd's cave...

It all seems rather obvious now, but it must have been an amazing moment when humans realized that circles are brilliant for moving things. Without circles the massive rocks used in building Stonehenge in Wiltshire and the pyramids in Egypt could never have been shifted into position.

But why circles?

Suppose you tried to roll a massive block of stone on square rollers, as the roller's corners went around it would make the stone go up and down. (That's if you could get it to move at all.) Anyone pulling would feel they were trying to haul the block up a row of very steep little hills! However, people soon realized that if they used round rollers under the stone, it would move along nice and smoothly.

The reason a circular roller works so well is that as it turns round, it will always keep the stone the same distance from the ground. That's because if you measure across a circle in any direction, the diameter will always be the same.

Rollers that aren't round
Amazingly enough there are other shapes you could use for your rollers and the stone would still move along smoothly. Just like a circle, these are shapes of *constant diameter*, but unlike a circle these shapes have corners! And just in case you're thinking this is some bizarre mathematical freak of an idea that can't possibly exist ... you might even have some of these shapes in your pocket! (Let's call these shapes with CONstant DIAMeters "condiams" for short. What fun! Anybody who hasn't read this book won't have the foggiest idea what it means.)

117

Here's how to draw the simplest condiam shape:

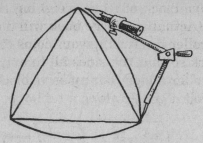

- Start with an equilateral triangle
- Stick your compass point into one corner and open the compasses to the length of a side. Draw an arc that loops over the opposite side.
- Repeat for the other two corners.

You end up with a triangle with curved sides, and amazingly this shape has a constant diameter because any point on one of the arcs is always the same distance from the opposite corner. If you roll this shape along, the highest point of the shape is always the same distance from the ground. If you had rollers that were this shape, you'd be able to haul your big block of stone smoothly!

Condiam shapes don't have to start with an equilateral triangle, you can use any regular pentagon, septagon, nonagon – so long as it has an odd number of sides. Some coins such as the 20p and the 50p are seven-sided, but notice how each side is slightly curved. The centre of each curve is on the opposite corner and so these coins are actually condiams! You can show this with a neat experiment. You need:

- Five or more 20p coins (or 50p coins if you're rich).

- Some Blu-tack.
- A massive block of stone weighing thousands of tonnes. (Actually, a large book will do).

Make a roller by sticking your coins together with the Blu-tack so that the sides all line up.

Put the roller under your massive block of stone or book and roll it gently along a tabletop.

Even though your roller has "corners", does the stone or book seem to "bump" as it goes? No! That's because your roller has a constant diameter! So thanks to a pile of 20p pieces, you can now go ahead and construct a giant megalithic circle in your kitchen.

Why do wheels always have to be circles?

The difference between a wheel and a roller is that whatever you're moving along sits on top of a roller. However with a wheel, you need to be able to fix an axle in the exact centre. Unless you want your car, lorry, tricycle, pushchair or train bouncing up and down, you must make sure this centre is always the same distance above the ground. That's why you need a circle – because only in a circle is the centre always the same distance from the edge.

The funny thing about condiams is that there is no "centre" which stays exactly the same distance above the ground, so that's one reason why wheels are not made in condiam shapes. Of course it's not the main reason – the *main* reason is that condiams would be a real pain to make whereas circles are nice and easy.

LUMPS AND BUMPS

We're about to examine "regular solids", which might not sound very exciting, but don't skip this chapter. If you pass regular solids without appreciating them, you're missing out on a treat. (Ask any old person, they'll nod wisely and tell you this is all too true.)

Regular solids have a very special place all to themselves in maths because they are in a very exclusive club – there are only FIVE of them.

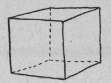

CUBE (OR 'HEXAHEDRON')
6 SQUARE FACES
8 CORNERS
12 EDGES

TETRAHEDRON
4 EQUILATERAL TRIANGLE FACES
4 CORNERS
6 EDGES

ICOSAHEDRON
20 EQUILATERAL TRIANGLE FACES
12 CORNERS
30 EDGES

OCTAHEDRON
8 EQUILATERAL TRIANGLE FACES
6 CORNERS
12 EDGES

DODECAHEDRON
12 PENTAGON FACES
20 CORNERS
? EDGES

Rules of entry to the Reg-Sol Club:

1 All your faces must be a regular polygon.

2 All your faces must be exactly the same size and shape.

3 Each corner must have the same number of faces joining on to it.

4 No trainers.

CAN I JOIN THE CLUB? ALL MY FACES ARE SQUARES, AND THEY'RE EXACTLY THE SAME...

Sorry mate, you're wearing trainers. And check rule three – all your outside corners have three faces joining them, but the corners in the middle each have six faces.

Let's just check we know what the different words mean:

● **Face** is what you call a flat side of a solid.

● **Vertex** is what mathematicians insist on calling the corner of a solid. So if ever you see a mathsy person slip over in the kitchen and slam his face into the corner of a worktop, remind him that what he *should* tell the hospital is, "I've just smashed my nose on a vertex." He'll be very grateful that you put him right.

- **Edge** is what you call the er ... edge of a solid. It's a line where two faces meet and it runs between two "vertices" – or between two corners if you're normal.

Looking back at the reg-sols, you'll see that there are three with triangular faces, there's one with square faces and one with pentagons. You can't use any other regular polygon to make a solid that obeys all the rules. If you did try to make an interesting lump by gluing together, for example, a load of octagons, you'd only end up with something looking like an old parachute.

Euler's amazing formula:
Whatever kind of solid you've got, so long as there are no curved edges or faces, you can say: **Faces + Vertices = Edges + 2**. For the cube this works out as 6 faces + 8 vertices = 12 edges + 2. It always works! Can you work out how many edges the dodecahedron should have? Check your answer by carefully counting on the picture!

The rule even works if you chop corners off or add lumps on. Try it out on this:

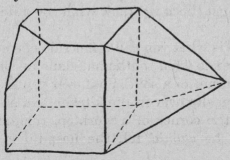

What have regular solids got to do with anything?

Although it's been known for thousands of years that there are only five regular solids, no one was quite sure *why*. It seemed so magical that everyone expected there would be a link connecting them with something utterly fabulous such as the tides of the sea, music, the ancient gods or even the whole universe.

Picture the scene: we're in Athens, Greece, and the time is about 2,400 years ago. There's a bloke called Plato who spends his time just thinking about *thinking* which is a very tough subject indeed. It involves Plato pulling the world apart and putting it back together inside his head, and as the people haven't got football or pop music or cinemas to entertain them, they're dribbling in anticipation to hear how he's been getting on. Plato knows about these five mysterious regular solids, so he's been sitting up all night with his scissors and glue desperately trying to think of how he can fit them into his big scheme of things.

124

WE COULD DO MATCHING ACCESSORIES LIKE BAGS AND SHOES! THEY COULD BE HUGE NEXT SEASON!

SHHH! HE'S ON TO SOMETHING!

PONDER PONDER

GOTTIT! THE UNIVERSE IS MADE OF THESE FIVE SOLIDS!

EH??

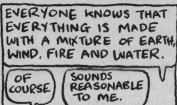

EVERYONE KNOWS THAT EVERYTHING IS MADE WITH A MIXTURE OF EARTH, WIND, FIRE AND WATER.

OF COURSE.

SOUNDS REASONABLE TO ME.

WELL, WHEN YOU THINK ABOUT IT, WIND IS MADE FROM OCTAHEDRONS, EARTH IS MADE OF CUBES, FIRE IS MADE FROM TETRAHEDRONS AND WATER IS MADE OF ICOSAHEDRONS.

YOU MISSED OUT DODECAHEDRONS

OH RATS. THERE'S ALWAYS **ONE** ISN'T THERE?

YEAH, WELL... IT'S OBVIOUS INNIT? DODECAHEDRONS REPRESENT THE UNIVERSE AS A WHOLE.

This idea was such a hit that the five reg-sols became known as the "Platonic solids". After all, it did seem to fit in with a few clues offered by nature because pure salt crystals are cubes and perfect diamonds are octahedrons. (It must have been a bit disappointing when people finally realized that things are made of different atoms, rather than fire, wind, earth and water. Imagine the fun you'd have if your trousers were made of windy fire.)

A couple of thousand years after Plato, another genius called Johannes Kepler thought of a completely different use for the five regular solids. You'll need to shut your eyes to imagine this.

HANG ON! Don't shut your eyes yet because you haven't read what you're supposed to imagine yet. Good grief!

Johannes was a brilliant astronomer, but at the time only six planets had been discovered: Mercury, Venus, Earth, Mars, Jupiter and Saturn. Johannes wondered why this should be until he hit on the notion that if there are six planets, there must be *five* spaces between them.

FIVE SPACES? AND FIVE REGULAR SOLIDS? I WONDER...

Of course this isn't as simple as it sounds. The planets are different distances from the sun and go around it at different speeds, so you can't just measure the distance between each planet as if they were all in a line.

Here's how he suggested it all goes together:
- Imagine the Sun in the very middle.
- Around the Sun is a large sphere with a line drawn around the circumference. That line represents the path in which Mercury flies around the Sun.

- Fitted around the outside of the Mercury sphere is an octahedron. The faces of the octahedron all touch the outside of the sphere. Then around the outside of the octohedron is another bigger sphere which touches all the corners of the octahedron. This also has a line drawn around the circumference which shows the path of Venus.
- Around the outside of the Venus sphere is an icosahedron, and then around this is an even bigger sphere with a line showing Earth's path.
- Outside Earth's sphere is a dodecahedron, and fitted outside this is an even bigger sphere which is the Mars sphere.
- Next there's a tetrahedron round the Mars sphere and then around that is the even bigger Jupiter sphere.
- Finally (how's your head doing by the way?) there's a cube round the Jupiter sphere and then a sphere for Saturn.

It's probably easiest to imagine how the Saturn and Jupiter spheres are linked to start with. Suppose the Saturn sphere is a plastic football and you chop it in half. You then find the biggest cube shaped box that will fit inside the football. Then you find the biggest ball that will fit inside the box. That ball would be the Jupiter sphere.

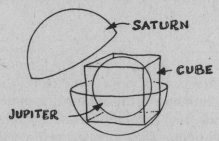

Got that?

Johannes' idea was completely away with the fairies which is a bit sad as it would have been a rather cute way of explaining why the distances between the planets are what they are. It's also sad because Johannes had a pretty miserable life, but at least his later ideas about planets and how they move were totally brilliant. You can read about them in the ellipses chapter. (In the end Johannes died in poverty, having spent ages trying to collect wages he was owed and saving his mother from being burnt as a witch.)

Nets

A "net" is a drawing of all the faces of a solid that you can cut out and fold into shape.

The easiest net is probably the one that makes a cube and here are four different versions. You could

128

cut any of them out and fold them to make a cube, but here's a little teaser for you: the opposite faces of a die should add up to seven. Which is the only net that would make a proper die?

It can be rather fun making your own dice, as you'll see if we pay a quick visit to the Last Chance Saloon. Brett Shuffler and Riverboat Lil are coming to the end of a gruelling all-night Snakes and Ladders session, and it all hangs on Lil's next throw...

130

As well as the normal six-sided die, you can make perfectly fair four-sided, eight-sided, twelve-sided and 20-sided dice using the regular solids. Here are how the nets look, so you can draw your own bigger versions and cut them out yourself.

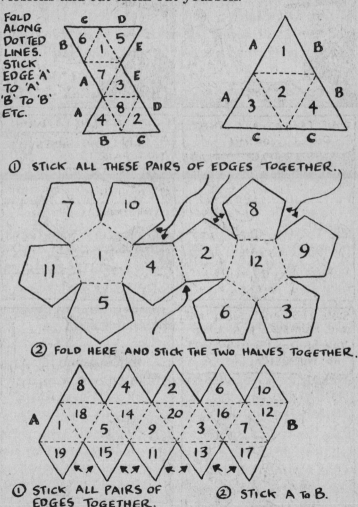

FOLD ALONG DOTTED LINES. STICK EDGE 'A' TO 'A' 'B' TO 'B' ETC.

① STICK ALL THESE PAIRS OF EDGES TOGETHER.

② FOLD HERE AND STICK THE TWO HALVES TOGETHER.

① STICK ALL PAIRS OF EDGES TOGETHER.

② STICK A TO B.

Note: the four-sided die always lands with a corner on top. So you need to throw the die on to a glass table and then crawl underneath and look up to see what number is on the bottom.

Other fair dice

You can make a fair die with any even number of faces. Here's what a ten-sided die looks like:

TOP VIEW

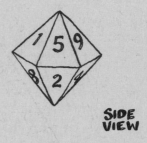

SIDE VIEW

It's like two five-sided pyramids stuck together at the bottom. In all there are ten triangular faces. These *could* be equilateral but it would make the die very flat, so they are usually taller and thinner. Even if the triangles were equilateral, can you see why this would not be a new regular solid?

Answer:
Because two corners have five faces touching them, and the other corners have four faces.

This die is like the four-sided die because it always lands with an edge at the top, so you need to see what number is on the bottom. If you wanted to go mad you could make some really fancy dice. How about a perfectly fair 34-sided die? All you need to

132

do is make two 17-sided pyramids and stick them together. It'd be brilliant for whizzing past somebody else's hotels when you're playing Monopoly!

Moons of Zog

The planet Zog has two unusual moons. Tinjx is a tetrahedron, and here's a complete map of the surface:

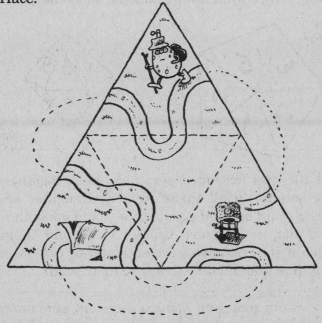

A lonely Gollark is on a camping holiday and has gone for a walk down Tinjx's only path to the well. If you cut out the map and fold it to make a model of Tinjx, the dotted lines show how the path links up.

As you might imagine, Tinjx doesn't offer much to a relaxing conqueror of the universe, but the octahedral planet Ptuon is more of a challenge.

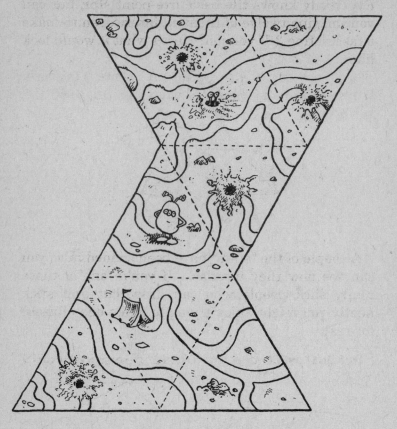

Can you find a route to get the Gollark back to his tent, but without going over any meteor holes? If you're clever you might be able to work out the route just by working out which edges of the map link up. Otherwise copy it out, cut it out and make your very own model of Ptuon. If you make it big enough you could even go camping on it.

Make your own superstar!

Everybody knows the basic five-point star, but can you imagine twelve of them all interwoven to make a fascinating 3-D version? Here's what it would look like:

A couple of the "stars" have been shaded in so you can see how they interlock. If you're one of those really slick people who can draw, cut and stick neatly you might enjoy trying to make one of these for real.

YOU JUST NEED ONE OF THESE DODECAHEDRONS

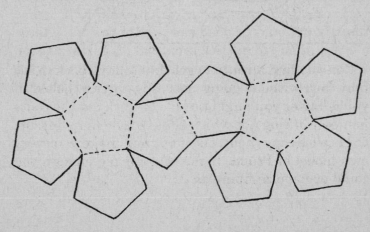

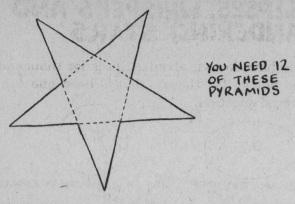

YOU NEED 12
OF THESE
PYRAMIDS

Make a large copy of these nets – including twelve of the pyramid nets.

- Cut out and make up the dodecahedron and all the pyramids.
- Stick a pyramid exactly on each face of the dodecahedron.
- Get twelve different colours and paint each five-pointed star. (Each pyramid should end up with five different colours on it.)

If you take your time you'll end up having made something truly amazing – and you'll be a superstar yourself. (Our murderous artist The Evil Reeve thought it would be dead easy but in the end a team of firemen had to unstick him from his kitchen table. Even then he walked around for weeks unaware that he still had one little pyramid glued to the back of his head.)

ELLIPSES, WHISPERS AND WANDERING STARS

People have known about ellipses for thousands of years, but so far there's always been one big unanswered question:

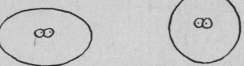

IS AN ELLIPSE JUST A SQUASHED CIRCLE?

We put this to our Murderous Maths research staff who have set up an experiment to tackle this vital issue for once and for all. Let's see how they're getting on...

And that proves that you can't just squash any old circle and get an ellipse. If you read the bit about loci on page 22 you'll know that a circle is the locus of all points equidistant from the centre. Here's the fun part – an ellipse is like a circle with *two* centres:

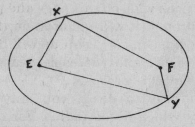

The first thing to know is that the centres aren't in the centre so they get called "foci" instead. (It's another of those words like "locus" where if you have one of them it's "focus" and if you have more than one it's foci.) We've called them E and F for Ellipse Foci.

The important bit is that if you pick any place on the ellipse and measure the distances to each focus, the two distances always add up to the same

138

amount. So the lengths of lines EX + FX add up to the same as EY + FY.

IS AN ELLIPSE LIKE AN EGG?

No, because an egg has one end pointier than the other and also you can't dip your little buttered toast soldiers into a boiled ellipse.

Ellipse measurement (the tough bit)

Every Murderous Maths book has to have a tough bit so that you can show it to your teacher or your auntie or your grandchildren and say, "See? It isn't all rubbish. This book is a valuable learning experience." Even if you don't understand this tough bit, open the book wide on this page and push it flat. Then if you drop it, it will fall open on this section. Anybody who happens to pick it up will think this is your favourite bit and therefore you must be a genius. Anyway, here it comes...

When you draw a circle you only need one measurement which is the radius. For ellipses you need two measurements. One measurement is how big it is, and the other is how fat or thin it is. Here's how they work.

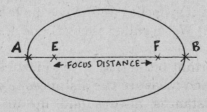

The "how big it is" measurement is the distance between the foci which is easy enough. On the picture it's EF. The "fat or thin" measurement is a bit tougher. It's called the *eccentricity* of the ellipse and to work it out you have to measure AB. You then make a fraction by dividing $\frac{EF}{AB}$ and this fraction is the eccentricity. Obviously AB always has to be longer than EF (you couldn't have the foci outside the ellipse, that'd be like having a circle with the centre on the outside) so the eccentricity is always less than 1.

Don't worry about the sums. The main thing is: the bigger the eccentricity, the longer and thinner your ellipse will be. On the other hand, if the eccentricity is very small, your ellipse will be round and fat. If your two foci are on top of each other then the distance between them will be 0, so the eccentricity will be 0. You end up with a circle and you can't get rounder or fatter than that.

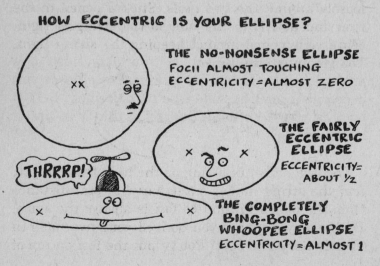

HOW ECCENTRIC IS YOUR ELLIPSE?

THE NO-NONSENSE ELLIPSE
FOCII ALMOST TOUCHING
ECCENTRICITY = ALMOST ZERO

THE FAIRLY ECCENTRIC ELLIPSE
ECCENTRICITY = ABOUT ½

THRRRP!

THE COMPLETELY BING-BONG WHOOPEE ELLIPSE
ECCENTRICITY = ALMOST 1

You've just got past the tough bit, now go and lick your face in a mirror you gorgeous clever person.

How to draw a perfect ellipse

- Chuck away your ruler and reach for a hammer and two nails.
- Ignore your compasses, and grab a length of string.
- Move away from the antique polished mother-of-pearl inlaid Louis XIV desk you usually work at and approach a carved-up old workbench.

Put your paper on the bench and bang the nails in through it. Tie your string into a loop which goes loosely around the two nails. Stick a pencil in the loop and pull it to the side so the string is tight. Move your pencil around keeping the string tight. You get an ellipse. Bingo!

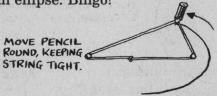

MOVE PENCIL ROUND, KEEPING STRING TIGHT.

The two nails are acting as the foci of the ellipse, and the string makes sure that the total distance from the pencil to the two foci is always the same. By the way, suppose you banged your two nails in exactly the same spot? You've put the foci on top of each other and as we said before, when you move the pencil round you get a circle.

How to fold an ellipse
It's strange – but it works!
- Cut out a big circle of paper.
- Mark a little "X" somewhere in the circle, but NOT at the centre.
- Fold the paper over so the edge touches the "X". Make a crease.
- Keep moving the paper round and folding so different bits of the circle touch the "X".
- Eventually all the creases you put in the paper will surround an ellipse shape.

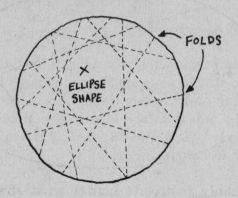

How to pour an ellipse
This is easy, but a bit useless. Get a round glass of water and tip it. The surface of the water will become an ellipse shape. (This also works if your glass has straight, sloping sides.)

Why bother with ellipses?

There are tons of ways that ellipses come up in science, but we've only room to find out about a few of them.

THE ELLIPTICAL ROOM

Suppose you have a room with an elliptical floor and a solid wall going right round the edge. You stand on one focus point and you get Binky Smallbrains to stand on the other. If you throw a ball *in any direction* it will bounce off the curved wall and go straight to Binky. If he throws it back the same thing happens!

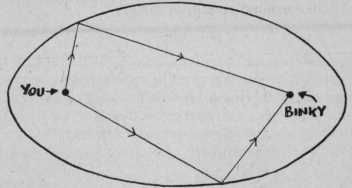

Incredibly, it doesn't matter what shape ellipse you have (fat or thin) and it doesn't matter where you throw the ball – the shape of the wall is just right to bounce a ball from one focus point to the other!

Be warned. It isn't only a ball that will bounce at Binky. Don't whisper anything rude about him because *every* bit of sound you make will bounce off the wall straight towards him, and he will hear you perfectly. If you don't believe it, then grab yourself a slice of culture by visiting...

THE WHISPERING GALLERY

There are several buildings around the world that use the ellipse effect, and probably the most famous is St Paul's Cathedral in London. The inside of the dome is an ellipse shape and there's a walkway that runs right round passing through the focus points. If you got a big knife and chopped the dome in half it would look a bit like this:

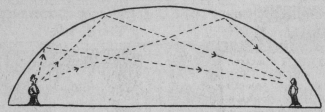

Because sound waves all bounce from one focus to the other, if there's someone whispering on the opposite side, you can hear them clearly even though they are about 30 metres away. That's why it's called the "Whispering Gallery". Spooky!

PLANETS

145

So what went wrong?

If the Earth did travel around the sun in a perfect circle, then the Gollarks' plan would have worked ... but it doesn't! Do you remember we met Johannes Kepler back on page 126? One of his bits of brilliance is that he worked out what shape the Earth really does move in:

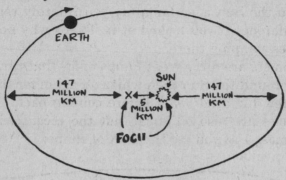

You'll see the Earth travels round a massive ellipse. We've exaggerated the ellipse shape here (in fact the Earth orbit is almost a circle) but the main point is that the Sun is *not* in the middle! In fact the sun is at one focus and even though there's nothing at the other focus, there is a distance of about 5,000,000 km between the two foci. This means that the distance from the Sun to the Earth varies between about 147,000,000 km and 152,000,000 km.

All the other planets travel in elliptical orbits too and, remember, the shape depends on the "eccentricity". The Earth's eccentricity is a tiny 0.017.

● Venus and Neptunes' orbits are even more circular than Earth's. Their eccentricities are 0.007 and 0.009. A bit boring really.

- Mercury traces out a much better ellipse shape. It's eccentricity is 0.206 and its distance from the Sun varies from about 46,000,000 km to 70,000,000 km. If you were camping on Mercury you'd find that some days the Sun would look a lot bigger than others!
- Pluto has the most eccentric orbit at 0.248. Mind you the Sun is so far away you'd hardly tell the difference if you looked at it. That's why nobody goes camping there.
- Comets are dirty great lumps of ice that turn up, fly round the Sun then whizz off again for maybe a few hundred years before coming back. Their orbits are also elliptical, but the eccentricity is almost 1 so you get this sort of shape:

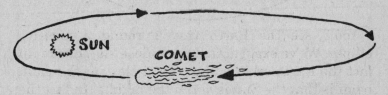

Incidentally, when the old Greeks were staring up at the night sky they thought that all the twinkly things were stars. However they did notice that most of the stars stayed in the same patterns, but a few of them seemed to wander about, so they called them "wandering stars". Their word for wanderer was *planetes* and that's how we came to call them planets.

There, wasn't that a great chapter? Not only did you take on some top maths, you also got information on cathedral architecture, astronomy and ancient Greek all for no extra charge.

PROVE IT, PYTHO!

What a shame. Once again we're reaching the end of a Murderous Maths book and yet there's so much more cool, amazing and downright weird stuff to find out. Of course, like any subject, maths also has its tedious side so as we've got a few pages left, let's take the chance to get revenge on someone who has given us many long centuries of grief. Remember how we started this book? Well, once again we'll push buttons 7, 35 and 43 and enter the Secret Vault. Prepare to encounter some *pure evil*...

M'LUD, COUNCIL FOR THE PROSECUTION, ACTING ON BEHALF OF MURDEROUS MATHS READERS ALL OVER THE WORLD, WOULD LIKE TO PRESENT A CASE AGAINST...

PYTHAGORAS!

And it's about time too, isn't it? For the last 2,500 years Pythagoras has caused maths fans some really murderous sums and stinky exam questions with his "theorem". This is how it goes:

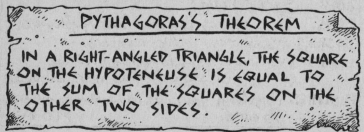

PYTHAGORAS'S THEOREM

IN A RIGHT-ANGLED TRIANGLE, THE SQUARE ON THE HYPOTENEUSE IS EQUAL TO THE SUM OF THE SQUARES ON THE OTHER TWO SIDES.

Yuck – you'd be forgiven for running away and shoving your head under a pillow and pretending it wasn't there. Unfortunately it IS there but at last we're going to give Pythagoras a grilling and see if he can justify lumbering us with 25 centuries of mathematical misery. Time to apply the electrodes and switch on...

The worms haven't eaten too much of him, so we'll give him a minute to recover, then get some answers. In the meantime, we'll check his file:

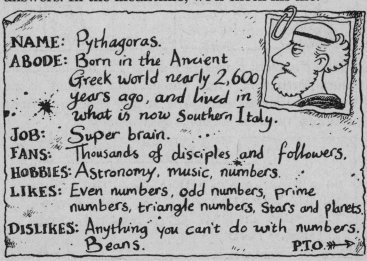

NAME: Pythagoras.
ABODE: Born in the Ancient Greek world nearly 2,600 years ago, and lived in what is now Southern Italy.
JOB: Super brain.
FANS: Thousands of disciples and followers.
HOBBIES: Astronomy, music, numbers.
LIKES: Even numbers, odd numbers, prime numbers, triangle numbers, stars and planets.
DISLIKES: Anything you can't do with numbers. Beans.

P.T.O.✱➔

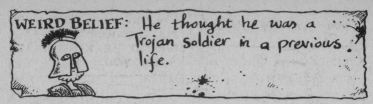

WEIRD BELIEF: He thought he was a Trojan soldier in a previous life.

The form carefully skips the fact that he was also a murderer, but if you can bear to read the grim details, you'll find them all in *More Murderous Maths*. Right now he's just shaking the maggots out of his ears, so let's quickly see what his theorem was actually trying to say.

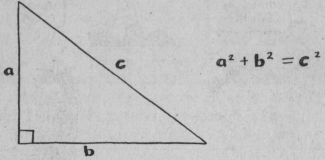

$$a^2 + b^2 = c^2$$

In a right-angled triangle, the "hypotenuse" is the fancy word to describe the longest side opposite the right angle. So what the theorem says is that if you measure the hypotenuse and then square the result (i.e. multiply it by itself) that should equal the squares of the other two lengths added together. Bleurghhh! The sooner we get him in the dock the better, eh?

IT'S PERFECTLY SIMPLE AND IT ALWAYS WORKS. I'LL MEASURE THE SIDES AND SHOW YOU.

151

Sit back, maths fans. It looks like old Pytho is about to show us some clever stuff, so let's give him a chance.

The first thing is to draw this diagram...

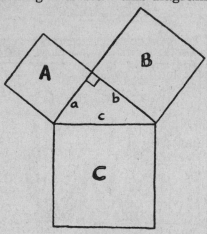

There's a right-angled triangle in the middle, and each side has been made into a square. Another way of looking at the theorem is to say that the area of the two smaller squares A and B together make exactly the same area as square C.

THE PURE MATHEMATICIANS DEMONSTRATE EXHIBIT B ON PAGES 46—49 OF THIS BOOK.

154

What a mess! But let's just pick the important bits out.

First, there's the right-angled triangle marked "ABC". You'll see each side has a square on it. We could have marked all the corners of the squares with little right angle signs, but it would look really messy so we haven't bothered. What Pytho has to do is *prove* that the areas of the two little squares add up to the big square.

The clever bit is the line AX which is the perpendicular that Pytho has just dropped. What he's done is draw a line from A which goes all the way down to meet the far side of the big square at a right angle. Pytho's perp divides the big square into two bits, and here's where he plays his master stroke...

FIRST I SHALL SHOW THAT THE RECTANGLE MARKED **PXZC** HAS THE SAME AREA AS **CARS**.

Pytho has also drawn a line between points B and S – we'll see why later. In the meantime here's his argument:

- Look at the triangle PXC. It has exactly half the area of the rectangle PXZC. Now look at triangle CRS – this has exactly half the area of the square CARS. (We can write this as $\triangle PXC = \frac{1}{2} PXZC$ and $\triangle CRS = \frac{1}{2} CARS$)
- If Pytho can show that these two triangles have the same area, then it follows that rectangle PXZC must be the same area as the square CARS.

- Start with triangles PXC and PAC. They have the same length base because they are both on the line PC. They also have the same height because lines AX and PC are parallel – so they must have the same area! (ΔPXC = ΔPAC)
- Now look at triangles PAC and CBS. We've separated them out and drawn them here along with the original triangle ABC.

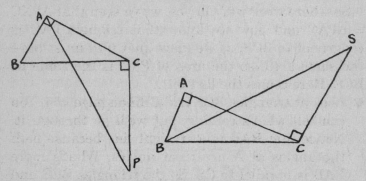

- Sides PC and CB are two sides from the same square CBQP, so they must be equal lengths.
- Sides CA and CS are from the square ACSR so they must be equal lengths.
- In the triangle ACP, the angle C is split into two bits. The bigger bit is a right angle (because it's the corner of a square). The smaller bit is the angle C in the right-angled triangle.
- Now look at the angle C in the triangle BCS. This is also split into two bits. The bigger bit is a right angle because it's the corner of a square, and the smaller bit is the same angle C in the right-angled triangle. Therefore the angle AĈP in the first triangle and the angle BĈS in the second triangle must be the same size!

- This means our two triangles ACP and BCS have two sides the same, AND the angle between them is the same. If you check exhibit A...

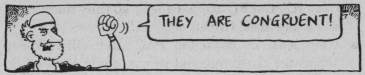

THEY ARE CONGRUENT!

Phew!

So where were we? Oh yes, we've seen that ΔPXC = ΔPAC and now we know that triangle PAC is congruent to BCS, so we know that *they* must have the same area, so the area of PXC is the same as BCS. Here comes the last bit...

- Look at triangles BCS and CRS on page 154. You can tell what's coming, but we'll go through it. Notice that RAB is a straight line because both the angles at A are right angles. What's more RAB is parallel to CS. So the triangles BCS and CRS have the same base and height and therefore the same area. Therefore triangle CRS also has the same area as triangle PXC, and so...

RECTANGLE PXZC HAS THE SAME AREA AS CARS!

ZZZZ

He's proved that the bigger rectangle has the same area as the square on the line AC. Now he has to show that rectangle QXZB has the same area as the small square, but the argument is exactly the same! Instead of writing it all out in full, let's do it in maths code. First you must imagine the lines AQ and BU and TC have been drawn in. Here we go...

$\triangle QXB = \frac{1}{2} QXZB$ and $\triangle BUT = \frac{1}{2} BTUA$

- $\triangle QXB = \triangle QAB$ (the triangles are on the same base with the same height).
- $\triangle QAB = \triangle BCT$ (they are congruent).
- $\triangle BCT = \triangle BUT$ (same base and same height again).
- Therefore the area of QXZB = the area of BTUA.

He's done it! Pythagoras has shown that if you split the big square into two bits with the perpendicular, one bit has the same area as one square, and the other is the same as the second square.

And so ... the big square is equal to the sum of the two smaller squares.

158

159